AUTOGRAPH EDITION

That Sweetest Wine
is published in a first edition
of 1000 numbered copies
and 26 lettered copies
signed by the author.

Copy *209*

That Sweetest Wine

That
Sweetest

THREE NOVELLAS

McPherson & Company

Wine

by Robert Cabot

Kingston, New York 1999

Published by McPherson & Company, Publishers,

Post Office Box 1126, Kingston, New York 12402.

Manufactured in the United States of America.

Typeset in Centaur.

First edition.

1 3 5 7 9 10 8 6 4 2

1999   2000   2001   2002

Library of Congress Cataloging-in-Publication Data

Cabot, Robert.
    That sweetest wine : three novellas / by Robert Cabot.
        p.   cm.
    Contents: Breath of the earth — A rat in the boardroom —
Touch of dust.
    ISBN 0-929701-60-7
    I. Title.
PS3553.A28T47   1999
813'.54—dc21   99-40262
                                                CIP

Designed by Bruce McPherson.
Printed on acid-free paper.

To
Giuseppe, Jimmy, Manlio

Breath of the Earth

Beppe

SHINING IN A ray of sun, our pirate's scimitar, half raised as if to slice off the bowed adoring heads, hilt black with time, the thin curved blade delicate death for unmutilated afterlife —it hangs against the white wall from a yellow cord fuzzed with mildew, from a spike badly driven, bent in the split plaster. Nearby stands our island's patron saint, arm lifted, offered to the cross.

I always sit in a certain seat—I raced there kicking up holy dust and frowns. I lean forward, as if eager for prayer, so that I make the saint's hand appear to grasp the hilt. How much better so, this righteous arm, than to have his shriveled relic lying on its velvet cushion in the silver case carved with cherubs! They carry it forth from behind purple curtains for the springtime procession, winding through the alleys. We boys of the village would have shoveled the cobbles clean of donkey dung, cursing to Jesus's whore mother under the sacristan's vacant eye, and the dung will stink again when it smolders under the soup pot. Did the arm stink too when they tore it, burned black, from the hermit's body —roasted suckling's foreleg on feast day? They'd sailed here with it, from his island to ours, racing from the unlucky ones. They had waited long, the old men say, for him to signal his death with the great flare of brush on his solitary rock, and then ripped him into relics as a baby will a bird dashed to death against the stone chimneys by the mountain wind. A charred root, that arm, sealed in the silver and glass.

I know about old men's hands, how they are never quite still, not like my mother's, quiet in her lap as she sighs by the cold fire. How they grope, and search, and beckon the past, clasp onto my wrist as if I were a threshing stick. And how the yellow knuckles are like knots on an olive cane. Every autumn, when the olives have done with their sweet work of sap and leaves and the fruit turns black, when the wood has shrunk and hardened against the wrenching winds and the ice, I make a walking stick for my grandfather. With the knife father gave me that always, now that I am finished with school, hangs at my waist in its goat-horn sheath, I cut just the right T-forked branch, carefully peel it, smooth the roughest knots, round the handle so it will fit his dry palm, calm his trembling. I turn it over flameless embers, slide it slowly back and forth, first one end then the other, until it darkens, tightens—but not too much or it will become as brittle as his bones. For a cup of oil, which I draw from our black chestnut keg, the blacksmith shoes it with a thick iron point. With the hard smooth end of a walnut stick I rub beeswax into it. It glows with a life of its own.

On my grandfather's saint's day, while he nods and his mouth slacks open, propped on his stone bench under the fireplace hood, I secretly replace last year's cane, its point gone, its end frayed and split. I wake him with the crack of the old wood, the spray of sparks, as I throw it on the fire. His eyes light. His hand weights my shoulder like a bone.

"Come, boy, the scimitar."

Only my grandfather is allowed by the priest to take it down from the wall. From behind the altar I pull out the steps the sacristan uses to hang the scarlet feast-day banners from their brackets on the columns. With ceremony, using his new cane, my grandfather climbs up, smudging the whitewashed wall with his sooty fingers, unties the curving sword.

For a time it seems warm in the church, holding the heat of women's bodies from morning mass. As he tells the story, though, sitting on the dilapidated bench, the blue cold slips in around my ankles, up my shins. I sit on my hands. The cold and the story drive my blood into a hot red center and I hunch tightly around it. My eyes follow the strange incisions on the blade of the scimitar, awkward in his twisted hooking hands.

It's a familiar story, I do not hear it all. My thoughts wind through his sentences... Grave markers in our cemetery with their brown enamel photographs of the dead. The great heap of bones in the crypt, discarded there from the oven tombs on the wall when memory dies... The Fountain of the Pirate's Blood... The marble tablets on the wine shop wall to the island's two heroes, both with my name...

"My grandfather told me of that day just as I tell you now. We sat here on this bench, this sword in his hands.

"He had gone off that morning, long ago, alone to the olives down near the sea where they were already ripe and falling from the trees. He knew nothing of it until he heard the bell and guessed. He'd left his wife and children in the village packing the last of the figs, dried in their ovens and brought in the day before in the donkey panniers. They were perched on the wide top of the wall, just beyond the watch tower they call Crazy Ones. When I was a boy I packed figs there too with my mother. It is flat and clean there, no better place in our fortress village, built here in God's grace with the steep rock slopes of the Pagans' Mountain dropping all around us. And they saw the black sails come heeling into the Cove of the Hawks. The screeches of the children and women rose up from the village like a flock of frightened crows. The bell began to sound. And my grandfather was down in the olives near where they would land."

Beppe's forefather

THE WIND scratches with the sharp points
of the leaves, the ground swings beneath
me through the black branches. The fruit
this year is meager, the basket at my waist
fills slowly. We shall not starve, they say, and our misery protects us, no one will take that from us. They
gave us the land and the village—that gave them nothing but debts. The winter wheat is tender still against
the coming ice, the rain would not let it grow. But
some will live, and it will be ours. That is all, no riches,
even our chalice is tin. Any treasure our fathers may
have torn from this thin soil has been taken from us.
Our great forest of chestnut, which brought goods
from beyond the mountains and the sea, was cut away
by the last lords, sold to the yards to make ships of
war. And she would drag me and the children to church
to hear that sniveling blue-faced one pray to this great
benefactor! May the saints tear him to pieces in their
eagerness to have him with them!

For months I'm in these trees, taking their fruit, trimming them. "The old wood bears no fruit, son," and
my father would point his fingers up around the cup

of his palm like the ribs of a pannier before we weave in the strips of split cane, to show me how an olive tree should be pruned, letting sun and air into its heart. These trees twist their limbs around me, stain my hands black-red, fill my eyes and my nose with their sawdust, drive their weight into my bones—and give me back oil and firewood.

I hear the distant sea. A hawk calls shrilly, I see him, watching, hungry. A snake weaves out too far from cover, a mouse or lizard stills its twitchings, sleeps in the autumn sun: death would be a feathered rush, black pain stabbing through, no moment left for fear. I have dozed on those ledges, there where we spread the grapes and the figs to sweeten in the sun. I have heard that final instant of death, seen the great wing shut out the sky, the talons close on a rat who had ventured out to steal my bread crust. The single cry and the leap and thrust and climb back to his cliffs. Does he call me now?

Some say that is the best death, carried off from sleep in one fierce swoop. Not I. I would face my death, be terrified by it, fight it, and accept it with the bitterness of all life. I would know my end, for there is no other life. If there were would we endure this, would we hunger so long for one feast?

My stomach gripes, the blood runs thin behind my eyes. I climb down stiffly from the olive. With a chunk of bread and a bottle of the watered wine from the second pressing, I stretch out on the threshing rock, leaning against the straw pad and the wooden frame of the donkey saddle. The wind is sharp, the contrary wind that will not come when it is needed to blow off the chaff, to clean the chick-peas as they pour through my fingers. The sun is at half morning, I cannot rest long.

Wine from those twisted vine stumps; bread from the blades cutting up through the earth, from the oil of these trees, from the salt we scrape out of dried rock puddles by the sea, yeast from last week's mother-dough in its pot; fire from this rosemary and thorn and broom.

My hunger's held off some, there's less of that acid bite. Bread and wine—to warm the blood, they say, to soften anger and weariness and misery, to tell the old stories again, to bring a melancholy song from the con-certina, to embrace with a moment of pleasure, to sleep.

In the cave of my sleep, I stir, and for a balanced moment I am both asleep and aware that I am asleep. A faint jolt, a sliding off again. Then I'm caught, drawn into the open by the clear distant tone of the bell. The sun is far before noon, there is no feast day or church day, even a death would not start the weary striking until we returned in the black evening. By its rhythm it is urgent, violent.

Hide the saddle and the empty pannier deep in the brush, the other half-full pannier crooked on my el-

bow, clutch cursing onto my donkey, coil in her rope as she stumbles off under my driving heels. She knows me, and perhaps the bell too. The oaths and switches are fierce, she jogs well up the steep path.

The meaning of the alarm strikes within my skull. Pirates, it must be pirates! This is not the season for fires. For an accident they would send a boy. Once, for a visit of the great lords and their ladies, they would call us with the bell, but we are rid of that. And we are not fishermen to be called in from the sea by the cannons and signal fires and flags for a coming storm.

While the first bell still vibrated in my sleep I knew it was a sea raid.

Pirates! Fools! Our only riches are sun and misery.

I see nothing on the sea, only a beetle of a fishing boat making out around Wing Rock. But the Cove of the Hawks, where they would certainly head as it is the only landing beach near to us, is hidden from me.

Gaining the ridge, the wind sweeps down on me, brings the tumult of the bell, distant cries, the smell of the resinous olive smoke from the last fig ovens, donkey dung drying in the twisting path worn knee-deep in the rock and the dust by the clamberings of centuries. And the sharp taste of fear. A warm, then freezing, spread of urine on my thigh—three ships anchored in the cove, just beyond the watch tower's range, their boats are scattered on the beach, and already moving up from the shore is a swarm of dark figures flashing in the sun. Even against the wind I think I hear their shouts.

We clatter on, heaving up the great rounded steps. Maddened and frightened, with some idea that it will delay their upward rush when they come upon the slippery mess, I clumsily pour my olives out, many of them lodging between me and the wet stinking hide of the donkey, and fling the pannier off into the cactus and brush. I slide off and race on, flailing at the rump ahead of me, grabbing the tail for support. They are rushing on below me, only a few minutes behind. Before me are the ugly gray walls, the yellow-petaled tower trembling under its bell, crows swirling around—the whole melancholy village crouches there stupidly.

The wine will be out abjectly on the best tables now, the mayor getting dully into his feast-day coat, the great oak gates slamming shut, screeching open, wavering like an idiot's jaw, the old people sucking their spittle, the babies chuckling or wailing for their stomachs. The women will be all folded into themselves, each with her own plans to meet this new despair: to the church, cuffing at her rebellious children; or mute slow rocking, waiting by the fireplace; or racing with the rats in the cellars to hide the best cheeses and the tablecloth and the images and the thin gold earrings behind the vats; or saddling a donkey left behind from the olive picking, strapping on sacks of potatoes, a cluster of chickens by their feet, idols and babies and a heavy useless wooden tub, to hurry silently out into the brush; or straining from the wall's top to spot her men out on the donkey paths and scream to them what they must already know; or smiling secretly into the sun and the geraniums, wondering what it would be like to be sold in the slave market for the sultan's harem. And a thin cold fog of prayer seems to wrap the whole.

I can see the one cannon still pointing high over the cemetery where it had fired months before in dutiful memory of someone else's dead.

Confused life mocks in that sullen pile of stone before me. I stumble frantically toward it. My heart cries out to my children and my island. In disarray, in tangles, in unspeakable love. They call us pigheaded, the foreigners. But they do not know what this means, this pigheadedness of ours. We know nothing and we know everything. We take nothing. We give everything, throw it recklessly into our final feast day when we crumble back into our poor earth. There is no plan or great reward. Our secret, like a lemon root brought here by fathers of our fathers, its shoots beneath the soil each season grafted to its branches then cut away to make the new plants. Our secret is protected in our hard skulls and in the black eyes of our women. It is that we know beyond question our limits, our final end. We know the fullness of our toil, the heavy pain of the struggle with our rocks and our earth, the cruelty of drought and deluge and fire and earthquake. And the final limit of death is always with us. Knowing these things, though, we cannot be taken and we cannot be led. This is why we can feast: smile and sing and love. There we can be generous, reckless. So we are pigheaded.

As I approach, the bell fills the air with its blows, irregular, the upswing a sound of effort, with the full weight of the bell ringer, then the release, swinging free, hurling its tongue. I am close under the walls now. I am squashed by the pressure of the bell's hammering. Its doleful thunder closes out the very light of the sky, blackly and alone, stunned. For a moment it is I, deserted, storming this savage screaming rock. All is hostile, threatening, barren about me, and I know not which way to turn in my terror.

I gaze up at the wall brooding darkly over me. Streaked with the stains of refuse, stinking, ragged with seeds growing in cavities on its face; rats crawl in the rubble at its foot, bold and threatening. Crows squawk and scratch among them, dusty, scabrous, feathers broken. And planted on top of this whole mass, like an alder wood spike growing in caked dung, is the bell tower, mottled, decayed, splotched with yellow and white and pink stucco, black mildew.

With the warning of a faltering note, it is silent.

The silence is a vacuum, a million crickets in my head piercing to escape. My skull cracks open, breaks into jagged bits in the rubble. The silencing of the bell means that those of us left outside have lost the race, that we should turn about and hide in the rocks.

"Come! Hurry! Are you devil-struck! The gate! Imbecile, the pirates have your ass by the tail and you sit there talking to the crows!" I grab her by the ear, drag her, glaring at me with her blue-white eye, through the closing gate.

The priest falls on me. "The cannon! The others have not returned. The pirates are already at the spring. I cannot do it alone!"

Angry screaming women are placing the bars and props to the gate. The jumbled little square is deserted, doorways, windows, stairways crazily climbing the stone walls of our houses, streets opening off narrowly like dark tunnels under arching rock buttresses and rotting wooden props—deserted. Yet there are eyes on us, running feet echoing flatly, thin croaking shouts...rancid bait in a flat-stone trap... Escape! They are all mad, pulling the cover over their dank tomb. Seagulls cry over us, urge us to die.

The sky, trapped in our roofs and walls, burns intensely... Our well-digger, sitting at the bottom of his hole with his bread and wine, can look up and see stars in the patch of midday sky... Here, there are birds and a white moon.

So the others have stayed out, hiding in the fields. Why should I and this scrawny priest be the ones to risk our necks to protect some women, children, old ones, and their cellars? My wife and children rush up, streaked faces, they sour my heart. Come, she cries at me, we must escape, out, into the cliffs and brush, and I shall go anyhow, and you stay here with your skull of rock, for all I care!

For a long instant I seem stuck to the paving stones. Three pigs, caked gray, black-bristled, red eyes, are backed in a corner, untended, half-wild, tusks flesh-hungry from the months of grubbing in the roots. A donkey wanders into the square, a blood-red geranium plant in his yellow teeth—the village watchman had planted it in the bottom of a broken earthenware oil jar.

In ancient times the heap of stones on the edge of the west cliffs was a monastery. In the fall of each year, when the nights grew restless and long, two monks, winners of the longest lots, would come into the village, a purse tied to one girdle, a late geranium blossom tucked in the other. After much shuffling and calculation and scratching of whiskers and belly, the coins and the flower were left on the chosen stoop. By nightfall the ripest daughter would disappear.

It is said that she must hold the blossom in her mouth that first night with the abbot to be crushed by his yellow face, perfuming the natural stinks. Delicate, an honor. She would appear again in the spring with the status of a marriageable widow. And the child would be well provided for.

One spring, though, on the day of her release, as the girl was climbing heavily back along the goat paths toward the noon bells of our village, bearing her bag and her great belly and her black pride, pressed down by our wet brown sky, with only the warning of the seagulls' screams as they swirled free of the earth, she was struck down by an unseen hand, hurled in the dirt and the thorns and the red rock.

When they found her—they had been hoeing on the opposite slopes—her eyes were smiling far away, a small dark pig ran jeering from under her skirts into the bush, her belly was flat as a spade.

An earthquake had shaken the village violently that morning. Rushing to safety, they had seen the monastery split open. Half of it collapsed inward in a great whirl of dust and cries. The other half clung to the top of a slice of the mountainside cloven free. For a moment it balanced there, high like a huge wedge of cheese fixed in the sea, cowled figures frozen on the walls. Slowly it tipped outward, falling, faster, a wave forming at its foot, white water rushing in behind, hoarse shouts of the monks, gulls mocking, twisting an eye ready for floating flesh. With a huge sucking sigh it was gone. Some say that they could see the abbot thrown free, a red flame in his teeth, that while falling wings spread out from his shoulders, carried him swiftly out beyond the horizon. Some say the wings were golden white, some say burning black.

Dry, hard like a pine cone, I feel my son's hand in mine. "Go! Damned horns of the devil! Tell your mother you must hide in the cellar, behind the stall, no, in the wine vat. Madness! It is too late to flee, so we must explode the cannon in their faces to assure us no mercy. Away!"

The priest's eye is wild. He looks through me, hooks the air with his blue fingers in a beckon, flaps on through empty alleys. I remember now, how he had watched everything so carefully that time when the sergeant cannoneer came to teach me how to charge and load and fuse and fire, ready to salute the arrival of our great benefactor, watched me as I practiced its aim on feast days, his eyes like bullet holes in his tight face. He'd sit above me on the battlements, bare shins like white roots ripped from the cold earth, silent, prayer book gripped between his knees. He is my cousin, but many years older, always the blue corpse, white in the black cloth, always the lump of his jaw muscle throbbing. They say that when he was a boy, when from his silent corner, perhaps, he watched the dancing ankles and the soft flying bodices, when the blood turned lumpy and the fever gripped him in the groin, he would take a flail to his naked back till the swipple was blood wet.

Perhaps it is thanks to our saint that we have not all twisted and destroyed the heart. Though we are hard, strike sparks like our hoes, we can join in the quadrille too, we know soft smiles, we can sing like the yellow oriole. Our saint walks with us and draws from us the notes of our cane pipes and the verses of our old ones. He is saddened by his God, he protects us from Him. A bit of skin and bone in our reliquary, a figure of olive wood and plaster and paint, but he joins us in the square for a glass of our liquor, distilled from the last pressings of the grapes, sweetened and smoothed with wild licorice. He can sit with us on a boulder at the foot of the monk's cliff in the Sunday sun, pulling eels from the green sea.

Our saint was born here. He worked in the fields, and in the winter he and his wife and his sons cut and hauled wood out of the forests that there were around us in those days—the straight trunks would go to the steward, the rest for firewood for the villagers. On feast days he led the dances in the square, and they say he could hold more wine than any man of the island.

One winter the plague came and it struck down his entire family. He was left alone and half mad. He took to sleeping in the fields and the forests, never leaving his work. He grew gaunt and bearded and yellow of the eye and he worked with a demon in his soul. Yet his olives shriveled, his grapes were few and gave a bitter wine, the trunks he hauled out by himself were split and knotted. As his heart dried, so did his fruits. He was consumed with the bitterness of his grapes. His struggle was to take back from the earth what had been taken from him.

Sometimes they would see him as they climbed homeward behind their donkeys, high on his cliff-top plot against the fading sky, motionless, black with the swirling swallows and the first bats, fist shaking at the sky.

Was he not like our priest? Were not their gods the same, hate and love crossed?

It was his child, his son, who finally freed him.

One day he was working on the mountainside, building a new wall above his failing vineyards, a terrace with deeper soil beyond the reach of the salt sprays brought in by the westerly storms. With a heavy short-handled hammer and a tempered spike he was splitting away huge chunks of gray outcropping.

Those who would cut stone die young. There's the searching for the faults in the stone, tapping for a deader sound, and a few trial strikes with the spike preparing the starting point. Then the great blows begin—the rhythm of the swinging hammer, the jumping turning spike, the smoky wisps of dust, the death-slow deepening. And this is but one of a long creeping line of holes which must be driven along the fracture line, to be wedged with the sledge, waiting for the final slight softening in the bound of the blows, the wrench with the bar as the split follows through. How many blows for each slab wrested from the mountain? And with each the aching weight tied to the muscles along the side of the arm, the poise, the eye grasping the splayed head of the spike, straining for concentration, watch, watch, with the blood still oozing from a black bruise, the crash and the sting in both hands, the shock in a swollen elbow, eyes' image jumping, brain curling from the ring and the jolt. A labor which drives your mind into a trance, which commands you against the searing sun, the dry tongue and empty stomach, the dying light.

Our mad one was consumed by this work. For days he had been hammering at that shoulder of the mountain, throughout the daylight, into the half-moonlight. Long since he had cut enough stone for the new wall. All he could gain now from weeks of this would be a few handbreadths of terrace surface. And the pile of rubble had to be carried carefully away, stacked uselessly. All morning the sun had been drawing up great clouds, arranged along the eastern horizon, mounds of bleaching wool on dark columns. We watch these storms carefully, instinctively, for they can sweep down fast on us, break on us, and we may have drying figs or grapes or chick-peas to get in. Yet even as the shadows faded into gloom that afternoon, as the olives turned silver and the sea was swept dark purple, as heavy drops slapped steaming on the hot rocks, set random twigs of the rosemary jumping, made dust-plumed craters in the new earth...the steamy scents of the summer's first rain, the grapes sucking up the moisture, the olive leaves uncurling, the fruit renewing, the night hunt by torchlight for the hundreds of snails appearing from the walls and weeds, cooked in oil and garlic, plucked out and into the mouth with a hooked cane sliver...he hammered on, lost in his mad passion. Quickly it was a sweeping drenching storm, thunder exploding near. He worked on. Dust streaked his face, crusted blood melted, the ring of steel and rock deadened in the rain, slippery, the oak handle twisting. With a blow the spike gave slightly, a crack sprang down the rock face, one more strike would free it. The hammer raised once more, heavier for the bound was less, high—and the hammer was torn from his hand, the rock burned in a great flame, lifting up before his eyes, and all was a scarlet blackness.

The thunder rolled on down the mountainside but he did not hear it. The oily smell of the lightning washed away with the white rain sheets, torn burned flesh was cooled, he lay still and his mouth filled with water running down the raw faces of the stone. Still steaming in a puddle of the rock lay the hammer, its iron head split open like a drying fig, its handle charred—the wrench of his raised arm, the terrible light of a thousand suns all about him, his muscles turned to stone, the flaming curtain drawn about him.

He was lying, warm, to the crackle and the sweet smoke of burning fruitwood, the roar of the torrent outside, senses flickering, dimming, clearing, clouding like a landscape shadowed by the southeast wind clouds ...warmth, but as something that wraps the mind, no awareness of body, no pressure, no comfort, no stirring.

His first effort was to open his eyes. But they were helpless, without control, they would not stir. They seemed weighted by some outside force, and gradually his mind settled to a will to raise his right arm and brush aside those weights. Pain, sharp yet far away along his arm, he lay still and the pain receded. But his consciousness had been stirred. Warmth spread, he became aware of his weight, and he realized that his head was resting on something soft that moved from time to time. A high childish voice came to him. He knew it to be his son's.

"Father, I have come to comfort you. You must not try to see me or to speak to me, and I shall be called back soon. I have been told to give you a message. It is this: 'You must no longer torture yourself and the earth. You must accept. You must recover in peace at home. You must give away the fields. For ten years you shall never leave the village, helping there, when you are able, with whatever needs be done. And you must regain the love of those about you.' Yes, those are the exact words. 'Ten years from today you shall take a boat alone to the Island of the Savior and there you shall live for the rest of your days as a hermit. Whoever shall come to you there, you shall care for and instruct in the ways of the earth, for you shall find that you have much to teach others, sending them back renewed and wise. When your work is done all shall know, for the island will burst into flame, and you will be carried to us.'" Gently his head was rested on a pillow of moss, and, though he heard nothing, he knew that his son had left.

He obeyed. Somehow he dragged himself to the village square, still blinded, half-paralyzed, with his seared arm. They were afraid of him at first, this wild and stricken man, but they helped him to his sister's hearth. Gradually as he recovered he re-won the village's confidence. In the autumn sun he would sit on a stool in the square, his arm bare, stretched forth with its angry scar twisting down its length, drawing the flesh taut. He would tell over and over the story of his sorrow, his folly, his hate, and his miraculous warning and deliverance. His story grew and assumed a rude rhythm and rhyme. Sometimes other men of the village would join him to the wandering notes of a shepherd's pipe, the verse passing from one to the other, weaving through the stories of our ancestors, our proverbs, our mysteries, our customs, but always returning to the miracle of the lightning and its lessons.

As the use and the strength of his hands returned they gained great skill. While the poetry flowed from him and echoed with the others circled there, his hands would be busy, weaving panniers of split cane and willow, twisting the golden straw and working it into chair seats, fashioning donkey saddles from oak and olive wood, forming handles for hoe and ax and pick, twining yellow rushes on paddle-like frames of mats for drying orrisroot, repairing the round grass pads of the oil presses, cutting out gourds and fitting long flexible cane handles to their necks to be used to fling water from the ditches up onto the vegetable plots, carving the swivel knobs on tough fruitwood sticks and tying them with hemp twine to make flails, making the moon-shaped rush buckets to be hung at your belly for olive picking. On warm evenings when the dark had come and the men were in from the fields, the square would fill with night blackened by the glowing tips of tobacco, with the murmurs and the movings of the villagers. Shufflings, glass ticking, curses, salutations in low voices, chairs settling on the paving stones. Spittings and snorts, the rush of a dog or an escaped child, a hoe striking rock as it is set aside, the steady rustlings of the grasses as a basket grew in the dark. A voice weaving proverbs, the notes of a pipe, the answering howls of a sheep dog. He showed us peace. He was one of us. He gave us a life whose struggle was not of opposites but of harmony, however hard, however deep the pain.

Still our old ones, in the evening dark or the Sunday sun, gather in the square to talk in that ancient poetry. The miracles, the proverbs, the loves and the deeds and the deaths of our people. We listen and learn and shall take their places...if we live through this madness.

It is good to see this servant of God sweat, struggling to swing the cannon around, dragging the powder box and the heavy balls. May it warm his God too, his frozen God. But this flapping crow of a cousin is right. To the cannon! This ball to howl at them, bounce off their skulls. And we shall shovel pebbles in the muzzle, make them hop. Wait for them to appear, just there, soon now. Above the sights hangs the Island of the Savior.

At the end of his ten years our saint left, sailed off alone in a speck of a boat which he little knew how to use. For now he had another task. He had returned his debt to the village, had brought peace and consolation. Now he would protect us from God.

The old verses speak of the sad patient Mother of the cycling seasons, the Guardian of the work of our hands, the Embracer of our sorrows, the Well of our joys, the Softener of our curses, the consoling Bosom for our bitterness and misery, the Womb of the gods that walk with us. So, before our saint came, She interceded with God. For us, God's disciplines are but hollow words, His wrath the twitching jaw muscle of a pallid priest, His judgments are washed in our rains, bleached with our sun, carried to the seas by our winds. Our songs on the evening air are our prayers, and it is our saint who must carry them, if he will, to God. That was his further task, sailing off from the Cove of the Hawks. He must leave us and learn His ways that he might represent us well.

And there he lived the rest of his life, far across the wind on that jagged mountain thrust out of the sea. Alone with the wild goats shipwrecked there generations before. They cared for him, clothed him, fed him, warmed him in his cave. Sometimes a fisherman, a passenger or two from the village, would visit him, bring him seed for his garden, a knife, needles, a hoe. And they would carry back his verses and many works of his hands.

On his hundredth year, his time came, came in the autumn when the grapes and the figs were in and the olives were ripening on the trees, when the earth thirsted and the winter hoeing and seeding waited for the rains. The ranks of storm clouds formed to the east, spread out across the sea. They could see from the village walls, waiting, how the first storm broke on the distant mountain island, the slanting gray of the rain against the black peaks, the shadow on the sea, the single lance of lightning. And soon there was a red wound where it had struck, the cloud lifting from the peaks against the white sky, lifting like a great stone slab, glowing over the flaming pyre.

When our villagers arrived in the swiftest boat, first among the several from other localities that had seen the miracle fulfilled, the mountainside was still smoldering. They found him lying near the mouth of his cave. The right sleeve of his rude tunic was ripped open in a charred tear, his chest was rent and his body seared. But his right arm was firm and smooth, the flaming scar had gone. His heart was warm and whole. In his hand was his reed pipe still moist from his breath.

Shouts from further up the wall. The pirates must be in view. Blow off the ash, the ember flares up, ready. My hands are cold. I strike out at the priest for his meddling, wrestle stupidly with the carriage. There, our target's there!

The touchhole flashes, leaps from under my hand—thunder, flame, a terrible jolt, the curse, the hammer crushing my head into my empty lungs, a black ball shrinking, fast, like a dog's eye in lamplight, hanging in the sky just before the heads of the yelling horde. A figure near the lead seems ripped in two, the parts thrown back into gaping yellow faces.

Black wine splashes in our mugs. The priest, who has returned from his mumblings and gesturings over the corpse, seeing to its burial there where it fell, is cheered. He looks angry. I am swung about in a wild dance to a pipe and a spluttering horn. My niece presses against me, soft with a kiss.

Beppe

GRANDFATHER SITS nodding beside me, his lower lip slack and trembling. Could such *1931* an old one have ever had a father? Musical notes cut in a marble plaque on the church wall near the scimitar decorate my name—or his name really, they gave me his name, my great grandfather's, our second hero. A hundred years ago he played his golden horn for the king and queen. They say he will trumpet the Last Judgment. He will stand with Gabriel, said the master.

The scimitar wavers in the wooden hand, but I am too cold to sleep. Two heroes in the marble, two grandfathers, the cannon and the horn. A brown spider crawls slowly in the cold along a crack in the stone floor, stopping often to feel cautiously to each side, resting, enfeebled by the urge to sleep or die. He approaches the wall beside the saint, stops for a long time at the angle, starts up the flaky plaster, crawls out on a rusty bracket, disappears into a glass cup with its two blood carnations from the widow's stoop box.

Like withering blossoms on his pale lips and white clipped beard, blood stains our hero. He died performing the annual ceremony over the grave of the pirate. They sent his trumpet to the master. We have nothing but the plaque and the pirate's grave.

My brother has taught me to make a pipe from a section of cane, this summer when we had swallowed our bread and cooled our stomachs with tomatoes and the threshing could wait till our father cursed at us. A slot and a plug for the mouthpiece, finger holes punched with a red-hot nail to the right intervals. And he has taught me to play. We play well, but he is the best, he always will be. I may have the hero's name but he must have more of the blood. He can play in the thousand voices of the birds, the south wind in the pines, the chattering of goats, the long ages in our village songs. And now he is gone. What could they teach him! He knows all the instruments, anything he could find and borrow. And he could play with the village band and even lead the quadrille on feast day. Two years older, but I shall not be able to do as much, now especially that he is gone and I must do his work in the fields, though my pipe wears a hole in my jacket pocket and mother will not patch it. But I have the name and I shall be the hero. They will see.

Pirates, music, what is there for me who must work forever in the earth to keep the pain from our stomachs? I rush off, only a shadow in the corner of my eye for the nodding old man—to our stone steps, the gray door, the empty smoky room. From the pot in the cupboard I scoop a bit of tomato paste, touch it to my lips and chin, throw myself on the cold brick floor, hold my breath dead. Crowns and thrones and courtiers, then flowing robes, turbans, crowding naked breasts, elephants, camels, a quadrille with my brother calling the sets and blowing six golden horns. Gabriel bows low.

At each tip, where the tendrils had been cut back before the winter, there's a gleaming drop, drawn forth by the early spring sun. I pick them off with my tongue, try to catch a flavor of the grapes, the earth smells of the spring hoeing. These bleeding wounds—I have tasted the blood of the cannon, of the burst heart.

Tomorrow is my name day and the day of the festival—the shouts and the band and the bright colors, swirling skirts, the taste of the spun sugar, the rice cakes. But it will be different, for I am thirteen now. I shall no longer walk in the procession with the women and children. I shall walk with the men. And I shall dance the quadrille.

My face and ear tips burn. My groin is a dark red pulsing as I kneel by the dripping vine. Curse the Virgin whore! Spring up, swing my hoe again and again, hard into the soft spring earth. Steadier, the regular rise and driving fall, the shining oak sliding back and forth through my hand, the grating as the heavy blade cuts into the rocky soil. My first hoeing, work of men, hard work, unchanging but for an occasional bigger weed to be chopped free and thrown into the brush or the torrent course between the terraces. I shall show them, I shall not stop and dream and idle as children do. He will not turn on me with his scorn.

The sun slants and the noon bell will not roll down upon us for many rows. Drive a hoe, drive a woman, they say—whispers, laughter, the sign of the fig. I freeze, a veil shuts them out. I would defend womanhood with a flaming sword.

Their scimitars swinging, they charged up this same slope, joining the mule track above. Often I have seen, though father laughs at me, the stain of the pirate's blood, and when I pass there alone I leave flowers in a crack in the rock.

They take me hostage when they flee, I sail away with them. I work as a cabin boy. In a sea battle I leap across from our masthead into the enemy's rigging as they are about to swing broadside with their superior guns. I cut their halyards, smothering them in great billows of canvas, their ship is helpless. By such feats I win their confidence, become their captain. We begin our mission of rescuing women from threats and insults, carrying them to a silver land where...

"The weeds work faster than you, my son! Would

you feed chickens with granny?" My shoulders strain and my stomach grunts manlike. In some of the cuts I make I see the white larvae of the cicada readying with the warmth to struggle forth and start their fierce rattling. I take care to turn them under again. They do no damage, for all their racket, their blind flights when you startle them in their olives, their spatterings of water as they crackle past you. I like their warning silences, the way they creep hiding around their dusty branches.

A spring snake sleeping in his new green skin is startled by my shadow, slides into a crevice, all but a hand's breadth of his tail, unaware, not used to his new length. I tickle him with a dried grass stalk and he flashes away.

I am hot to bursting like a chestnut in the coals, tired so my head swirls and the sky darkens. I cannot continue, but I do. I can no longer count the rows or look for the hawk that cries. The big weeds lie turned in the furrows, "We shall stop now. The noon bell. After our meal you will go down to the cove to gather snails and urchins to bake on the beach tonight with your friends. It is feast eve."

My feet hurry down the donkey path, through cherries and figs and the pale blue rosemary blossoms, the yellow dragon-head flowers of the broom. The great south wind flies me on, rushes past me, sweeps wrinkles from the smooth golden sea below me, out to the whitecaps beyond the sun. My body thumps along, soles slapping out little clouds of gray dust, slipping in the donkey dung where the glittering flies buzz angrily at my ankles, heels banging on the stones, jolting my cheeks so the horizon jumps.

There are other me's. I divide into pieces, scatter about here and there till I do not know which is real, which will be cursed. My heart already has me half in the cold water, naked. My legs are shorter, gray-green, bent beneath the surface. They could not be mine. My hands straighten when I take them from the sea with a snail pulling himself shut. My fingers reach carefully in between the urchin's black-red spikes. But my feet are still in the dust, my toes stretch out by themselves, seeking support on the steep path.

The brush is high now, almost closing in over my head. Long white thorns reach out, tigers in the jungle. Reptiles spring through the branches. Rustlings, chatterings, the green smells of spring, the rotting, a slug's slime.

The wind flies by above, but here it is still. I squat on one heel, a knee under my chin, waiting for something, stilling the whistling of breath in my nose. A shining eye flickers, blinks once, and is still. A tail trembles and is still, the withered green hand poised in mid-step. The sun draws back.

With only the warning of the hush and the pause,

nearby in the brush there is a curious silken sound, like our village standard unfurling when we carry it in the procession, the hollow beating of the wind catching the ragged silk, snapping it over our heads. I feel my heart slip away into my stomach, for it is she, our queen, the white owl. Very cautiously I turn my head toward the sound. Through the screen of stems and trunks, white like the quartz in our rocks, I see her just as her wings fold back. A flail's length away, squat on her feathered legs, her great eyes are fixed on me, flat, yellow. Without fear, the eyes hold me, draw me in.

It is I now, looking out through those solemn eyes at an ancient world of forests without man, onto time, onto great distances. I see a world without words where the owl and the snake are at peace and are the all-powerful, where their stillness commands the sun and the sea. I see them create weak shivering man, watch him with pride as his hands find skills and his head finds reasons, with pity as his heart falters and he seeks gods in his own image. I see them reluctantly choose a woman as their representative, as goddess for man, when she drew sweet oil from the bitter fruit of the olive.

And I hear her story sung on the winds that swirl in the village square. How her father was jealous of her in the womb and changed her ripening mother into a fly, swallowing her down with a draught of wine. How she was nevertheless born, thwarting him, enraging him, springing forth with a cry from his ear, full-grown, dressed in a goat's skin, a cock at her feet, a serpent coiled about her arm, a flowering olive sprig in her hair, and a white owl perched on her bare shoulder. How she triumphed over the sea god in their contest to be our people's god, he with his shining spear driven into the barren earth, bringing forth a cool stream, she bearing the olive with its miraculous fruit. Water we can gather from the skies, oil we must draw from the tree. Water cleanses, oil anoints. Water refreshes, oil is life.

How, when man became blind to his origins, became willful and would upset the balance of the earth, she protected the owl and the serpent from him. The cock at her feet instead would give himself to man, would crow his betrayal, and be thrown into the feast-day pot. How she guards our mothers, our silent sons, the work in our fields and our shops. How she is bathed in our tears and our sweat and our laughter. She asks only for patience and respect. She is at our heart.

So they sing.

Within the damp peeling walls of our church, where the incense mixes with our sweat and dead tyrants lie under our feet, it is Joseph's day and his flowers are pale and sad at the altar. I carry a pennant of the bleeding heart on a pole. Down the aisle and out into the spring sun, we drone the empty sounds in the gay alleys. My white surplice is stained gray from the grease of the rice cakes. Our boots poke out under our black skirts. And there are shouts and laughter only a few doors away from the lowered eyes and pudgy gestures of the priest. For out here it is the day of the owl and the goddess.

I scratch myself under the skirt and the bleeding heart sags, straightens when I am kicked from behind. Torrents of a donkey's sweet urine splatter as we pass his cellar. He screams for water or potato meal or a curse. Mothers watch us go by, cross themselves as if to seal in something under their hard knuckles, silent lips moving. Daughters, with their feast-day dresses protected under their school aprons, slipped on when the organ let them leave church, are held close, still guarded from the owl and the serpent by crooked hands —yet with glittering eyes.

The sea is as smooth as oil in a vat, the cellar candles are the stars. It stirs with the restless movings of the monsters in its depths, licks the beach, slides the stars about. The salt in the fire makes a million explosions. We juggle hot shells in our fingers, scoop out the meat with our knives, throw ourselves in the warm sand, shielded from the dew by the fire, and our heels float up over our heads in the fumes of the heavy wine.

...The tips of her long dark braids stroke me. I whirl

her by the waist through the steps of the quadrille. And then she is bathing with her sister in the rocks... The fever makes me sick until I must throw myself into the stars to escape. The March sea strips everything away. I turn back for the shore in mid-flight, groping for the bottom, wishing the crabs away, rising out in a sheet of the sea like a tuna with a dolphin on its tail, wrapping howling in the sand. Three at once bury me in an instant. In the warmth my skin loosens, and I laugh in my tomb with my head on a pillow of sand.

The moon, like a bruised overripe persimmon, lies fat and squashed beyond the black teeth of our saint's island. Bats chirp about us bug-hunting, dodge awkwardly across the moon. Foam hisses in the sand, like oil in the skittle, after each reluctant wavelet. The regular single whistle of the scops owl thickens the darkness as the moon disappears.

"Weren't you scared of her, being that close? They say her eyes are so big you can drown in them. Did she call?"

"She only calls at night, when the ghosts are out."

Somehow, all together, our eyes are in the fire, in the embers, and we are heroes dreaming of our feats. Through the red smoke I see the castle walls, cannons flashing, soundless screams of the fallen enemy. Maidens with blond hair. Mountains of miraculous harvest from the dry earth.

The fire flares on a seaweed pod. I see a boy put a cane pipe to his lips. The fire and the heroes fade. The notes are thin, drawn through a star-hole in the sky, the distance is so far, so lost, notes from another time, not of heroes but of ancestors sorrowing in other lands at the departure of their people, calling them back to the old ways. The sand presses in on me, hardens. A fear grows in my heart, I twist and thrust with all my strength. The piper has stopped and a wild cry rings like an echo from the rocks behind us. The others' eyes are on me, I am free, the sand falls from me.

Yet has not the owl found peace? Why am I afraid?

Feast day morning, the bell has been ringing since dawn, limping a little in its rhythm, louder softer as the ringer shifts, sometimes even missing a stroke. There is something about working the bell rope which dares you to keep your attention to it. Ever so gradually you are lured away until suddenly you are startled by that awful gap of silence. You hang with all your weight on the rope, and the ringing lurches on again. Today, except for a few such gaps, it will ring on and on until only a few minutes before the first event. No one would stay longer to ring it, miss the races, the contests, the dancing, the wonderful drunkenness, the lights and explosions, the stolen kisses, the hurdy-gurdy, the midnight fireworks, and how many other excitements which we have waited for the whole year through.

So it hammers and bounds and booms in our stone streets, in our houses, into our cold wet cellars and our stone skulls. It is voice among all voices. We need no persuading, but still the bell insists and insists, drives us on to greater excitement. And the whole village is turmoil. Arguings, unheeded women's screams, donkeys braying for attention. Men, trying to be casual, yet flushed and shining in their white shirts and dark jackets and insisting in supervising everyone else's preparations. Dogs, pigs, goats, chickens, pigeons, cats racing through the streets like the women's screams.

"Genuine, genuine, genuine, dressed in genuine silks, made from the rarest woods, eternal paints from the orient, dolls from the centuries of southern skill. Look, little miss! Is she not bigger than you, and almost as beautiful? Hold her tightly or she will waltz away with you. And you may have her, for nothing! Is that your father, yes, the one with the kindest face, the wisest face? Just ask him to take this ticket with its magic number, for just one thin coin to buy my donkey a bit of hay. Does he not deserve it, carrying this fairy doll to you from so far? Good! Crumple it, roll it into a ball, pop it into this turning cage of fortune—hold your breath, wish and the world is yours."

Hands and feet alone are not enough to win the pole-climbing. Next year they must let me, and I'll show them, I'll win. Already I have practiced on the great pole in our cellar where we winch the wine and olive press. Greased it with hog drippings, scooped a little at a time so they would not miss it from the soap-making. Ankles, knees, thighs, elbows, even your jaw twisted around slimy wood, straining against your belly, your groin, your chest. Then wriggling, inching, a spiraling motion. I can do it, I shall be the hero of our village quarter. Instead, this boy, red to bursting, has gained scarcely a handbreadth. His eyes are afraid, he trembles, we have lost. Cursed stupidity that they would choose such a fool. One must be a fool to lose so.

First I must see everything, watch the vendors as they stir their mixes, refill their glass jars, turn their spits and prod the charcoal embers, hold forth their cages and their bowls of golden fish, call out their extravagant promises, whirl their pinwheels in our faces, wind their somersaulting monkeys. But I know where my one coin will go. She will be there as she always has been, even way back when I was a child. With her mustache, of course, and her new-moon mole with the long crinkled hairs. How often have we dared each other to pluck one away with us when we pay her the kiss! Her enormous steaming breasts are held together with one perilous safety pin. Her blunt fingers pull magic from the hot syrup, like a sluggish over-fed bristly spider crouched in her web, her victims knowing the price yet lured to the joy of her spinning threads. Perhaps this time I shall see how she works her magic, how that burst of snowy dew-dropped sweet cloud on the end of a little stick can come from her bubbling pot. Twists and magic turnings, a mysterious bowl which she whirls and whirls, leers and mumblings and a far-off crooning. Heavy flesh, trickling with sweat, airy white billows form all about her under her great green umbrella.

Last of all I shall go there, claim my sparkling spun-sugar, hurry with it carefully to my mother. She will be sitting on the stone balustrade which borders the square on the side where there are no buildings, where it drops off sharp over the crows and the rubbish, over the rocks, to the sea. She will be happy and sad in her eyes. She will have taken nothing for herself from the coin box hidden under the wedding lace and the black weeds of her grandmother. And she will protest and laugh and pull free a bite and look proudly to the other black women about her. And I'll race away with the rest all stuck to my face.

Or must I grow up? Must I dance the quadrille with pale simpering girls when I could be out striding in the brush with my owl?

Now for the donkey race. Yellow dust and bits of manure fly back into my face with the cheers and roaring laughter of the crowds. Through it I can see just ahead the bouncing donkey rump and the blue and white silks of the Crazy Houses rider. I can never catch him. I do not care, I am glad not to be the hero. I even hardly remembered that I was to ride, and had to dash home for my colors and the banner with its painted fortress. Donkeys were not made to run. They will try sometimes only because they like to appear mean, like to rattle one's teeth, to drop droppings at the feet of the mayor. Now we are rounding the last towered corner of the walls, entering the square. "Crazy Houses! Crazy Houses! Crazy Houses!" I must finish, keep our angry donkey from stopping dead. We jog on, finish under the red and white streamer. Ignored, we stand watching the bustle about Crazy Houses, the banner of the owl awarded, the rider carried off on shoulders. I am glad I am not there, better left alone.

A distant pounding within the village walls begins, a regular beat. At first it is not something you hear; you feel it, deep in your chest. Then tootlings and clashings through the open portal—the village band. Our band is a marvelous thing, a special gift which you need not share. It is a kind of miracle. The dark stones and silent walls are given voice, they dance gaily to the music. The flowers on the stoops brighten. The grape-must smells from the cellars sweeten. I am carried like foam on the glittering waves of the music. And the bandsmen, men of our village, when they draw on their black jackets and caps with the dull golden braid, when they are assembled, when the fingerings, squeaks, toots, and rumblings are silenced, when they swing forth with their feet blinded and their faces darkened with effort, when their hearts burst forth with the explosion of their music, then they are as of different race. Almost gods, untouchable, grown huge in pride with their heads in the echoing clouds.

My brother would talk of military marches or a hero's song or a chorus of ancient high priests, but to me there was no such meaning. Each piece is specially mine, it starts within me. Walking beside the band, I possess the music, it resounds in inner places, fills my lungs, and spills the high clear notes into my head. Others can see the music, its gestures and effort and its colors of yellows and reds. Only I can contain its magic sounds. And when the music has quite filled me up, it lifts me, hot air in a paper balloon, carries me off.

So I swing along beside the band. There will be quite a way to go yet before they form in the middle of the square for the quadrille, winding within the walls, gathering its wake of children, out through the portal, then into the thicker crowd. As if they had waited for me, I look up into the flashing horns, waving their propped sheets of music like little banners, up into the swirling air over the proud march of the black caps. I am borne away on the chords and clashings.

For an endless instant the music is the burning rush

of the sun and wind pressing on me like an urging hand as I lie on warm grass by a cliff's edge. I dream to the slice of hawk's wings soaring below me in the streaming air, to the waves' steady drum roll far beneath where the wrinkled sea chews and froths angrily to bring me down, to the hawk's cry and the fisherman's cry, each hurling curses at a lost catch, to the ringing in my ears and the surge of my heart. I balance gently, ever so lightly on the edge, then throw myself free into the honey billows of the air.

Or the music is the moon, drawing me to it whirling like a twig thrown down a deep well to the silver circle of water. I fall straight into its heart and rest there suspended forever in the cool light.

The music is the lonely notes of my pipe. I lie in moss, propped against the curved base of a shading pine. My goats move eternally without command, from pasture to bubbling spring to new pasture, bringing me milk and cheese and wool coverings when I will. And I play till the gods are envious.

But the instant ends, leaves me dry and hollow as gourd, ready to be crushed into dust. The band has re-formed in the center of the square, the crowd moves back from it in a great circle, couples move forward, disorderly in the din of excited voices. And it comes to me in a great collapsing clap that I must dance too. She has discovered me, stands in front of me, takes my hand. I am cold and angry. I can feel my heart stop as if it would die rather than touch her. Women's world that saps and drains and sucks you away from the sun. And my feet are in the dust, my eyes follow swallows in the sky.

Laughter blinds me, presses on me till I feel nothing, not even the motion of the dance, splits open my head so the music and all sounds fly off to silence like cicadas from a shaken pear tree. Yet as cold can burn, as pain can finally break your nerves and release you, I do smile and my heart does beat again.

And later. It is darkening, time for the goddess call. Wild and forlorn, round and deep as if coming from a cave bored by the winds into the heart of a far cliff, echoing itself with its long drawn double note, the great white owl calls from the dark side of the twilight. This is her day and she would not have us forget. I walk carefully down little paths between vegetable gardens, straining over a sloshing bucket of water for our pig. The jumble of festival noises has withdrawn to a murmur. The bats have taken the sky from the swallows. I can smell the dew on the green shoots in the seed beds. The chill drives the confusion from my head, the clamor of too many people scrambling over me to win or to sell or to be admired, to lose themselves in a frenzy. Now I have muscles and heart again. But the serpents still sleep in their winter holes.

*   *   *

Autumn comes early up where the crags strip mist from the south wind, where the vines grow deep green, tall as my reach, in the cooler earth, where the fruit clusters fill with thin juices, bursting skins. These bunches are filled so tight you can't pull free single grapes without crushing, squirting blood-red. So we bite into the clusters, dripping from our chins.

In the lower vineyards, where the sun for five months has weighed on the earth, the grapes were smaller, loose in their clusters, distilled yellow, sweet as honey of the heather flowers. Down in the cliffs far below the main paths, where the ground is so steep and rough that rather than struggle the long way back up to the donkeys, dripping baskets strapped to our shoulder, we lowered them into a fishing boat tied against crunching barnacles at the base of the cliff. From there the boat would carry them to the cove where wagons hauled them up to the village.

My hands are sticky, the sweat pours down under my shirt, my feet in their ragged canvas shoes burn in the rough-hoed sods. All about is the coming and going, the tired afternoon murmuring of the other pickers. I see their leafy shadows working up and down in other rows. Occasionally another will appear as I am emptying my hand basket into a pannier, but there is no idling, we hurry back, women too, and the uncles and cousins who have left the land—a stonemason, a shopkeeper.

Working opposite me now, on the other side of my row, is my father. To favor me I know that he is taking the high and low bunches, leaving for me the easiest. It makes me angry. I work furiously to get ahead of him, to take my share, my side of the row, however high or low. "You work well, son, and you learn well. When these vineyards and fields are yours you will care for them and they will care for you." He takes his gray sweat cloth from his back pocket, dries his neck, starts again with his snipping and tossing of the clusters into the basket by his feet. I move my basket further along and am glad to see no other figures nearby through the rows. When my father speaks there is no room for answers. "This is a rich harvest, the richest I have ever known. The new vineyards have come in now. But you will not see it again like this. There's a weakening in the green, a yellowing in some of the leaves—the root disease, I have seen it today, and our earth is too shallow to replant with the stronger deep roots. Soon we must find other crops and go on. Once we were all woodcutters. The earth owes us nothing, it only collects some of its debts."

I hear the stories sung again into the night. Of the time of the forests, when homes were warm and dry with the wood, when there was fresh wild meat, when the summer sun was shaded, when the rains stayed in the earth and the winds were softened. When the gods lived close by. Shall our children sing of the time of the grapes?

The others have gone ahead with the donkeys. Mine is the last basket, black grapes from the eastern rows. The sky flames behind the swallows. My father squats waiting by the last pannier. He will carry it on his shoulder padded with burlap, up the steep path.

Snail shells crush loud under his heavy feet, he climbs slowly, avoiding the slippery sand. I carry the small baskets and the shears. We are silent, my thoughts close in under the weight of weariness. The smells of the brush, the sweet grapes, the foaming donkey urine, are fainter, the sky is going and I see only the worn forms and colors of the path, my feet lifting, thrusting back. I think of nothing now but the cold splash of water over my head, down my back, trickling under my belt and down my legs, the clean cool shirt.

The long table stretches outside our door where the alley widens, ready with last year's thick amber wine, *vin santo*, sweet from the special grapes spread on the ledges to absorb the autumn sun, with toasted bread spread with paste of chicken livers and anchovies and herbs, and fresh bread in torn chunks, broth, rice, sweet tomatoes, oil, cheese, and the great bottles of bitter white watered wine, glass after glass.

Mother pushes me into bed beside my brother. I lie carefully along the edge under the rough sheet. It is like the touch of a snake to have his buttock hump out against me as he rolls in his sleep. Bed boards squeak on their iron frames. A donkey calls halfheartedly, knowing it is too late to hope for attention tonight. A shutter clatters closed across the alley against the night air. As I often do, I slip out of bed to swing open our shutter and, with the dew drifting in from the cold stars, I hear faintly the double note of the owl calling from the forests.

T HE ROCK WALL of the Pagan rises heavily behind into the bright mist. Its top is lost, and further down too it sinks into the whiteness. Suspended, removed, in a strange between. Winter lies in balance with spring, fog burning cold with the sun, silvers, grays, blacks. A single great oak stump still stands, bone-hard old as the rocks, in the thin-washed field where only figs twist and jerk awkwardly in the wind. Crippled elbows, the abandoned.

19 57

When the forests had gone and figs were planted here, they say that at first they grew as large as chestnut trees, drawing on the forest soil and the opened sun. Now every year they dwindle, rendering less. The rocks cut through the earth, the Spring of the Brothers runs dry. Clean out the rotting wood, cut the cracked and broken branches, prune back and back that the thin sap may not be exhausted. My father's hands, cramped and twisted with age, strong like knots in an old trunk, work on, carefully, methodically, conserving.

By his will, his concentration, his special care, he seems to be showing me again, as if I were the son of twenty years ago, to be preparing me. He is silent. The pain in his hands and his knees cuts his breath and brings grimaces. Down by the sea there would be sun which would ease his rheumatism, or he could be sitting propped in the fireplace, as grandfather did, the warmth soaking into his bones. No, hard-headed as a tombstone.

This is only my habit, to wake to the blackest cold before the dawn. There was no special sound. The wind has stilled, the chattering of the bats outside the shutter is softened, soaked in mist. Behind the partitioning curtain—musty, and I picture its faded pattern of ladies on horseback led by their grooms through a slender forest—the old ones stir. Though I know already the creep of age through my veins, that curtain is a wall of rock protecting me from the rattlings of the unthinkable. As a child I strained to undo bed sounds —the grim creakings. Now I tense against the feverish cold tremblings, the whimperings and gases and fear— the abandoning.

"The moon is new. It is time to start on the grapevines." He sits close to the revived fire, half-turned from us so that we shall not see the trembling of his hands, the hot milk and coffee that spills from his lips, the weariness of his eyes. "You start the trimming today, tomorrow we can bring the wood up with the donkey."

"And you will stay here." She is angry.

"I shall take the donkey, finish the fig grove, bring back a load of firewood."

"You crazy old man! Obstinate as a rock! You want to kill yourself with work to bring us misery! You sit there shaking like a poplar leaf and say you're going out into this fog to hack at a few dying fig trees!"

"Do not be angry. Those figs saved our lives three years ago." Hail had torn our grain to nothing. That winter we lived on figs.

To his sharp curved back thinly covered with a gray bagging undershirt, frayed suspenders, jerking in a silent cough, I say "But we can finish that later, when the weather clears. We need not hurry with pruning, the sap will not start for many days yet."

Only the three of us now, my brother long since gone. For a time we are silent. Mother sits now with her face deep in her hands. He turns to us. Tears are running down through the creases and the white stubble, they glisten in the firelight. His hands are steady on his swollen knees.

"We have a custom in our village of hiding the worst. May it be damned! I am dying and I will not die here! My life is in the fields, that is where I will leave it. You shall not drag me to a deathbed—your hospitals, where you are shut off from the earth, where the air is the stink of rotting bowels, where they suck your life away with machines. With these hands I have drawn life from the earth. I will go back to the earth."

We remain sitting. He draws on his boots, rises, buttons painfully into his quilted jacket. His back is straighter, his step steady, as he moves slowly past us, resting a hand first on mother's shoulder, then mine. The door shuts behind him, cutting off the cold black breath.

My mother raises her face, streaming tears, toward the images on the wall over the faint oil flame. Her hands clutch white into the black cloth over her breasts, tearing at her despair. She makes no sound.

I—my heart grips at the dropping of the latch, and follows him. Down the stone alleys, echoing silence to the shuffling of hoofs, dawn darkening the roofs through the mist. Out into the worn tracks, the smells of the gardens and vineyards and groves that pass unseen. The breath of the earth.

* * *

I
9
7
7

IT IS Sunday, the bells call in the distance. They mark my time. It is an effort to break step with them. They have authority, but my path leads away from the village. Twenty years ago I carried the corner of my father's coffin out to the cypresses and the faded oval portraits, I stepped with the bells. But this insistence…

It is a peaceful place, our church, when the bells are stilled, cooler in summer, warmth lingering in the winter winds, a boy or two in whispered tricks, an old woman resting her misery, black skirts rustling about their business without interfering. I can rest my head on my arms, and I think our chipped and splitting saint with his dusty scimitar will not mind that I have none of their words on my lips, nor their gestures.

Why am I here, out in my dying fields? To measure the white moon—fertile seedings, ripenings, drought. To put off return, return to my father's anger still echoing from so many years ago, return to the stink of the donkey's stall, to the blue potatoes without oil or salt, to the never-ending scorn of my wife, so gross I cannot get near her, so bitter rank. Or to forget a donkey's split hoof, a long lost invitation for secret embraces, my spring hay ruined by a rain. Or to watch a fly winding round and round in a shaft of sunlight.

Beyond the mountain's shoulder the bell is swept away by the south wind, the village disappears. The brush thickens here and is taller—half-mockingly we call it a forest. Under the rushing wind I am closed into a hidden world. Riding on a donkey I could see out to the rocks and the sea, sounds would be drowned. Here, walking, I have the birds—nightingales screeching, the squawk and thumping of a pheasant, the cuckoo clucking like a chicken—the green smells of grasses and thistles hurrying to flower before the summer death, frightened lizards and black snakes twisting away. Closing in on me, holding me. How many times I have come this way to close out the present, to look away, to listen to the breath of the earth!

I step into the open, high over the circling hawks and the sea. My bones and my heart are stiff, I can no longer throw myself out on the warm grass, unite with the earth in embrace. In weariness, I sit, propped against a crumbling rubble wall, my back to the sea where the fishermen come no more.

Terrace upon terrace stretching out to the saddle, stepping on up the black peak, lie abandoned to the weeds and goats and brush and summer fires. Where once at this time it would have been green with the vines as far as you could see, running right down to the sand, and everywhere the click of the hoes and the cries of the donkeys—now abandoned. Crows—what is there for them here, what use their despairing cries?—crows, they deepen the distances, echo the emptiness. I am foreign here now, rejected. This cliff will split free and hurl me into the sea—vengeance of the earth. If it but would!

I shall stretch out—though where the warm grass grew is concrete debris now. Embrace, stiffly. Their guns needed shielding from the sky: a domed bunker long since tumbled into the sea, shielding from the horizons, slitted walls in rubble about me now, this pavement crumbling in weeds.

Where is their war now, and all their promises—elbows linked on the road to happiness? But I had my promises too, and where are they? For I believed what I wanted to believe, that we lived in misery and that there would be progress. Hopes! That is what they gave us—and they destroy us. The land strangles: vain labor, scorn, despair.

In the valley the morning shadows gather down to the sea, and across, high on the far shoulder, I can see the gray dead limbs of the figs where I found my father, where the great oaks once grew. Will there be anyone to find me when I go out to die? For I shall stay. It is they that are mad, not I, though they shall prevail. Did he somehow foresee this long losing struggle when he went out through the mist that last day? Were there portents even then? Yet he used to say, long before, that the earth gives as it takes away, that there is cycling of the fruits of the earth, that a crop may die away but another will take its place. Where is his new crop now, here where the brush closes in, where the sea is empty but for the whine of tourists, where the owl was driven away in terror and the harmless snakes are murdered and the venomous—never seen before—slide among our rocks?

Far below me is a single palm tree, its shredded leaves struggling in the south wind, where once there was a prosperous grove. Abandoned to the strangling brush and the winter storms, helpless as the last fishing boat slides off the sand, rounds the headland, and puts out to sea, never to return. As the house turns silent, its windows black sockets, its bones burned white in the sun and the salt air. As the sea foams in over the indestructible litter of their plastic amusements. There is his new crop!

But I shall stay, however bitter the anger about me. Perhaps it is mad, perhaps they are right. There is no hope here. Oh! it is true that those of us who remain argue and propose plans to save ourselves: we will build roads to our fields, kill off the hoarding rodents, rebuild our terraces deep against the root disease. But it will never be, and our sons instead will surely leave. Already they learn the new ways from the strangers, how to soften their muscles, scorn their fathers, cover themselves with vanity and become bookkeepers, waiters, factory men, priests, perfume sellers, pimps. It is good, of course, they must go, there is nothing here for them. But it is a dying to me, I see no new life, I cannot understand. And there is so little time left to us here. That is what I fight, the closing in, the withering of time.

She taunts me that I could sell my land to the foreigners for fortunes and leave forever this life which she calls miserable. Join their fat and greed...ancestors, heroes, saints...how does my story end?

The old men and the idiots (she calls me both), we walk the earth still, though the paths close in on us. Among the falling terraces, the weeds, the thorn bushes, there are a few vegetable plots, vineyards, fruit trees, olives. We have some defenses: stones propped on trigger sticks, baited for the rats that gnaw through the grain stalks till they topple and the ripe fruit is stripped away, wire snares on the rabbit runs, swaths cut through the brush around the fields to break the summer fires— mostly caused by the tourist horde. Each year there's the weakening of the vines, the thinning of the bunches—yet the golden grapes, now hardly bigger than beans, give a few last barrels of brown wine as sweet as honey, as strong as brandy. Each year we must harvest the grapes earlier, even before the first autumn rains can replenish them, to keep them from the devouring rabbits and the plucking pink tourist fingers. Figs rotting on the trees, chick-peas to the pigs now—their tinseled candies and powdered soups mock us.

Resist, but have no hope. Stay, but the mothers and sons will go.

"You wonder what I do here? I am waiting. I am old, the arthritis has twisted my legs, I can no longer work. There is no one left to take my place. You know. Her sons, the last has gone now. He called me a fool, screamed at me that this land is worthless, that he would no longer hack his life away for a few kegs of wine. And he went. She tells me to at least stay home where she needn't worry. But I would die here with my earth. Till then, I sit in the shade of this pine, I eat a few spring figs—there are enough still. Here. And I watch my land."

He unties his knotted handkerchief and hands me three figs, black, sweet. He continues hammering at pine nuts with a stone.

"The summer mist is darker this year—over the sea where the sun sets. They say it is like an oily poison in the cities, their explosions and burnings and wastings."

So this is where the old one spends his days. I rarely see him in the village. Bare feet, rags—his sons took everything—but his legs are as straight and strong as mine. I shall be silent. It is not my concern.

"It is mine, much more than theirs. Who is it that has cared for it all these years, never leaving it to ruin—like all that? And he would come here with his great belly and his wheezing lungs loading down the old donkey who hasn't carried more than a basket or two of wizened fruit for years. They say it took two of them to even get him up on to her. I wasn't there. My brother, who hasn't been out here since he left to join the police force forty years ago! Swilling our wine on feast days, lording it over us. Then, when there's talk of land being bought by the foreigners... That stranger with his eye-glasses and camera and his strange way of talking. And all the time I'm sitting right over there, behind that rock where there's shade in the morning, hearing every word of their bargainings... But they cannot throw me off. The surveyor will tell you that it is mine too."

He has taken out his horn-handled knife and is paring and digging at his toenails. Beyond him, over the glossy white sea—the morning wind has gone—the form of a tanker is suspended in the haze, throbbing silently as though the sound came not through the air but through the sea and the rock.

"So I am waiting here for them to come again. I must watch for them every minute. I have no time, no strength left, to struggle with the weeds and the brush now. I share the fruit that still ripens with the lizards and the birds and the rats and the rabbits. And I can tell you where the hawks nest and how the shadows shrink and stretch and slide out over the earth."

That single pine where the old one dozes out his

life, it hangs high over the sea, an hour's climb up, a twenty-minute descent in the days when the paths were clear. My feet work better than my head at finding the path—once a boy Sunday fishing. At first steep down through boulders, almost a cliff, then the old terraces and water runs, the stone huts stinking of bats, the ground torn by the wandering goats and the half-wild pigs. The brush thickens, thorns tear at me, pricking me with their poison, charred stretches blacken my legs still wrapped in dust cloths from the early-morning hoeing. A cicada rushes from a wild olive tree, striking hard against my ear—a startled screech, droplets of his cold moisture. Blackberries snarl, thick with their white flowers. I move through stands of ragged uncut cane, grape roots hooking out among the thistles. I sit for a time in the shade of a ruined hut by a lemon tree split and dying. Once again, though, its leaf, crushed in my fingers gently, gives its fresh green-yellow scent of fruit. My mouth runs sweet...Her face was clear and smiling and her breath was the ripe lemon fruit and everything was to come...Roaring motors fly behind the sun....

Finally, breaking out onto boulders, the sea is at my feet. Green in the calm between the smooth waves—a dead sea, we call it, coming from some storm far beyond. It's as deep as the cliffs are high, down to the sand and the sliding black ledges, my sunken treasure ships. A sea where I too shall never float again. For how could I, even though they are far from here? Their smooth brown bodies, their indifference, their laughing scorn. They have taken the sea away from us. My sons learn their ways, I cannot.

It was two hours from the village even when there were paths and one could find them. No, they could never make their way here until they build their road, their panoramic road. Peace here, a deep rocky cove where the sea washes clean, unreached by them. Here our boats would tie to a natural shelf to load the grapes, carry them around to the beach for the wagons.

But they are here too. Soft tanned bodies and the pink ones, shouts in foreign tongue, a motor yacht screeching forth music, the masks and fins and bombs and harpoon guns, picnic papers drifting off on the tide, blond hair—they have come, bringing their world here. How generous to offer me their iced beer! What riches! Their diversions: amuse yourselves well!

So I turn back from the sea, from their calls and wavings and blue eyes, up through the granite blocks and steep ledges where steps had been cut for harvesters' feet. Into the cactus and thorns, up onto the top of the cliff which forms the south side of the cove, to get them out of sight.

Our walls that we built in other times were solid. We built for all time, just as we planted trees and laid out our vineyards. Yet the weeds tear now at our work. One of the three long narrow stones built into the wall as jutting steps has fallen out. Its socket is a tangle of wild flowers.

For a few years I had kept up this vineyard, working it alone when they abandoned me, resisting. Now the vines struggle yellow in the weeds. My friends, I had to leave you, your fruit, to the lizards and the mice and the sparrows. No one passes here now. No one takes or leaves. The few figs rot and are nibbled away by the ants. For a year or two the vines climb back up their cane fences, then these collapse. The thistles, the wild grasses, the blackberries reach out over them, the final seasons pass unnoticed. The little beasts and bugs too will forget, will turn to wilder fruits and seeds.

On that flat stone by the spring, which will have been sucked out now by the rank rushes, there will be a sickle I abandoned, broken, years ago, undisturbed, honed then rusted thin as a wire, the handle a cracked gray bone.

Here there are no paths, only the ruins of our vineyard, the water courses impassable with growth. Yet beyond our last wall, dropping down to the leveler far end of the broad headland, is the solid green of healthy well-kept vines, a hut freshly white-washed, the smell of burning rosemary twigs.

She's almost black except for her wild white hair

swinging to and fro, seated there, slumped forward, a load of dung dumped there, a white chicken scratching at the top. I shall not disturb you. Sing your droning song of the pirate Redbeard carrying off the maidens of the village. Your head is raised, your arms reach out to sickle the dry grass in a circle about you, in a circle about the vineyards and orchards and vegetable plot. Your head drops again into rocking dreams and madness.

Among the vegetables near the hut I see thin arched buttocks bending in the young tomatoes, the creased white backs of knees, the stretched skirt, rolled black stockings, boots. No motherhood softening, no child rounding the hips, nor any man thrust wide those knees. The dry one. Leather, unsmiling, we rarely speak to her or see her in the village. From the first hoeing until the last harvesting she stays out here in her fields, sleeps in her hut with this mad one.

"A visitor! An idler. Ah yes. But you have come too far and too late. You have grown gray from the hard little boy who scrambled behind the wall, threw rocks at the rats. You have lost too much. There are no paths back where you have come from. But try my peaches, they will be weeks ahead of yours. Go on, take it, I have not poisoned it."

"You too have gone far. But I see that you have come back to scare off the crows... Not bad, your peach."

"Off with you! No, come back. Sit there under the

fig and reset this handle, young man. You may throw the sun away, not I. She there has mixed my seeds together to feed her raven and I must sort them for the late planting."

"It is possible, cutting here and tapering. But it will come shorter by a hand's breadth...so time whittles at our bones, bends our backs, until we are at the other end of the spade...this hard earth...few come back to it once gone."

Her eyes, close together making a sharper point, pierce into my skull, seek hostilely. Do not fear me, old woman, I am not here to mock you. I am as much a friend as you will find in this world.

"You weren't a bad boy. What are you doing here?"

"It is a long time since I have been out here, on this side. I would see our land again...sometimes it is better to look back...there is nothing ahead. They are leaving. My sons, the women. Anger and insolence, sloth. Protected by their church. Mocking me...It is Sunday, the tourists and the land agents will be looking for me, scheming, wanting to take my land from me. The yachts will be swarming off my rocks, laughing, stinking so the snails and urchins I gather taste of oil, telling me work has no end...Today my legs led me here, tomorrow I shall begin again...Why? I do not know. Because they are wrong, mad. Because the earth is the source, money is nothing. Because I am too weak to try their ways. Because I am a fool. I do not know why. But why have you come back, why do you stay? I have heard it said that you have been offered millions for this headland, enough for you and your sister to live without work wherever you will for the rest of your lives."

"You do not sell and you do not know why. For my part, I know. And I shall tell you. There are not many of us left. You were a good boy. I would have someone know. There is more honor in the truth than in the evil tongues and the twisted lies which hiss about me when I return to the village. And no one else comes out here now, sits with an old woman, though you do gibe me."

Her eyes have faded. Her fingers scratch among the seeds spread on a rough baked-earth washing tile on her lap.

"Truth sorts lies. Lies feed the ravens' tongues. She was mad from the day she saw, from her secret cave with her dolls of sticks and scraps, her father lie down in the brush with a woman not her mother. They saw her wild eyes staring at them in the midst of their embrace, saw them move back into the darkness. I was born from that.

"For many years I lived in the rages and black silences and strange loves and hates of those two families, half-guessing their cause. The others—my father's wife, my mother's husband—must have known soon, perhaps from the rambling talk and madness of my half-sister, for that is what she is. The village is small, but the secret was kept. No one thought it strange when, at fifteen I started working in my real father's fields. He had only that one daughter in his house, his wife was ill. I could be spared for there were many sons in my mother's house. I was paid something for my work—that was not unusual.

"We left when I was twenty, the day after my real father's wife died. And that was when I learned the truth. She had been ill a long time. It was the custom for neighbors to come to visit her, propped up in her bed in the dark corner, on Sunday afternoons. That last Sunday it happened that my mother, my supposed father, and I called on her when she was alone with my real father and this poor creature. Perhaps that was the first time we had been all together like that with no one else. Wisdom of the crazy. My sister was squatting at the foot of her mother's bed. When she saw us come in she started screaming. 'There she is! There she is! Who drew the devil out of my father and sank it into her belly! And this girl is what came out! His eyes! His eyes! My dolls! Save them!'

"So the wound of honor was ripped open. The two men could no longer pretend. They were too old for killing, though perhaps it would have ended that way if the ill woman had not died in those first minutes.

We had noticed nothing, caught in the silence which trapped the two men, until there was a stirring and mumbling in the corner. The crazy one had crept up to the head of the bed and was trying to close the slack jaw and the fixed eyes of a dead woman.

"With no word spoken between them, it was understood. For the summer heat, the funeral would be the next morning. We would leave that afternoon—his mad daughter, and me as the servant girl. His brother had already been urging him to take over his small business and his house in the city, as he had had a stroke and would be for the rest of his days in a cure home. I would be paid, would take care of the two.

"And that is what happened. For twenty years we stayed in the city. And your tongues here wound out their webs of lies about the widower and the pretty young servant girl, who already while they were still in the village and his wife was still alive had been. . . Then he died, leaving everything to me, this mad one too. And we came back to our land.

"For that was what my father willed. And he was right. The earth is truth, the rest is hate and lies, the tongues of ravens and lizards. I need no longer hear the voices and the laughing. We shall die here one day and our ass will return empty to the village to tell you.

"Do not tell me of others, of strangers, of tourists you call them, do not whine of the past, of your sons, of other fields and lands. All of that matters not, is but morning mist when the sun is low…This dust, this handful of soil, was once the granite rock, yet the sweet fig springs from it…The rest is as nothing.…

"They used to say in the city that those who work the earth are of the basest sort, the meanest of man. My father would be silent to this, but when he was alone with us sometimes he would sob like a child, curse the devil in him for driving him from his land. He would teach me the ways of the earth so that when he no longer lived and kept us in exile we could return and live under the sun and the wind."

"Your walls are high, old woman, and your days are short. Yet you have learned well. I shall remember your story. When your ass returns there will be one who will know.

"Those cicadas singing. Their work is done, their eggs are planted in the earth, they have shed their old bodies. In their new clear wings, veined like the skeleton of the India fig, they cling to stalks and branches, eating nothing, taking nothing, waiting for death. Yet they sing, for three months they sing, until they have shaken their hearts out in the sun and they fall empty of their last song for the ants to carry away…I understand you. I shall remember."

"Go with God."

"Go with God, old woman."

From the waves of heat and the heavy sweet scent of the brush, I stop in the thin shade of a dwarfed and dying chestnut tree where the cooler air flows down a narrow gully like an invisible brook, where to breathe is to drink. A cicada only an arm's length away almost hidden in the gray bark, quivers his belly—perhaps his emptiness resounds, makes his mad cry ever shriller as he nears death—his vibrations penetrate, ring quite within my ear, directionless, clear like a bell inside my skull.

Below, the wandering melody begins again:

> O brave Redbeard fly! Steer the eastern sky!
> Take me far and on and away.
> Where the wine is sweet and our lips will meet.
> Let us sail on swift and away!
> Let us sail on swift and away!

A few old tin cans and plates and night pots still hang from fig branches, bang faintly in the breeze, scaring no sparrows from the black-burnt terraced slope. Higher, dry greens and browns again. In the steep solid ledge running up between banks and holding-walls winds a groove shin-deep and but a hand-span across, worn by a thousand years of asses' hoofs, clumsy for straddling or tripping boots, slippery with a trickle of slime: the last life of the Spring of the Owl before it sinks away.

On I climb, higher, through a stand of cane, rattling and sawing in the wind, forgotten, the patch of a threshing stone in the brush, to this grape-pressing hut, its single window shoulder-high with a rounded ledge to rest the panniers, its stone spout at the base pouring into the half-circle open trough for the foaming juice—now a bowl of yellowing thistles with their dry purple blossoms. The sea, hanging down from the sky, is a burning yellow-white sheet, hot haze...cold mist drifting through my father's fig trees, the pruning...black goats move fast through the sparse feed of the brush just at the rock line...in the crushing grip of the afternoon heat.

The half-hidden valley of the Owl hangs high in the folds of the Pagan, the Joseph tree is in flower for its name day, the leaning pines spread out to shade their roots. Here the circling wall is piled high with thorn branches against the rabbits, and here a ruined carved stone portal, broad with winding steps where once sedan chairs passed they say, up through terraces of deep-green grapes, tomatoes, eggplants high as your breast, beans and gourds and herbs and onions and the waving heads of last year's celery flowers drying for the seeds, ditches channeling the spring water back of each plot to be thrown with half-gourds on cane poles into the green when the sun sets. And here the shading medlars and giant chestnuts and sorb apples, the voice of the water dropping into the first pool from its dark cave, changing patterns of floating leaves and frog's eggs and lily pads and water bugs, the cold shock at the back of my neck flooding down my face and off my hair and nose as I bend under the stream, fresh greens crowding about to escape the shivering heat of the dry abandoned hillsides.

"Good evening, friend. Try this cucumber for the thirst. They are as sweet as watermelons this year. You are far from your fields today. It is a long way to go only to call on the old sisters. You cannot walk past on this slope of the Pagan without my seeing you. And how shall your wife know?"

He is proud of his steel teeth, given him in military service, grinning wide.

"You can change those to gold now, with your millions, and fix up this old ruin, Lord Goldentooth of the Owl—until they hiccup in the city and your money vanishes. Then where will you be?"

"Ai! Do not build and ruin me yet. Though I sold my lands by the sea I still have this. And I shall keep it. They shall never find it, here more than an hour from the village and far from the sea. I shall bury myself yet in the old fellow's graveyard behind his chapel there—and it will stay in ruins. The millions disappear with my sons—I shall be lucky if I see any of them again. Yours are not old enough yet, you do not know what it is like. It will come. It will come."

I try to tense my heart, my lips are weak…images blurred, colorless…hostile silence, the images of my three sons behind a wall of glass, heads lowered deep into soup bowls, my tongue swelling in fear…Weeds: my fingers numb, the sweat pouring into my eyes…The winds, the great wall circling our village, the screaming crows, the whirling sun—our kitchen is dark, the figures fade behind a wall of dust…A sliver of sun through the ferns which arch out over the black of the spring's mouth gleams gold on one of his teeth.

"They will stay, never fear you that. They could not break my will." No, it is good that they go, it is right. Misery, that is what they say—go! Brave Redbeard!

The heat…faint, unsteady…the world tips up behind me to spill me into the sea, white through the nodding leaves below…only a friend, familiar words …or hunger, or fear. But the voice trails on. An ant winds through the thickets of hair on my crooked hand. I screw tight my stomach to belch, it will help.

"Steady, friend. Do not say too much. They watch the shows in the evening, the bar…prizes, shining suits, the undressed girls, rewards and all so easy…plastic squeezed into every shape, waxed marble. To sleep on the earth floors of our huts, to hoe for fifteen hours with water and bread and a half a dried fish, to measure the ruin every morning from the rabbits while the wardens collect fines for the snares and post bulletins on our walls for the outsiders to see about the hunter's autumn paradise... The clients swim naked, the fishermen say, lie about on the rocks with bottles of oil and their boxed screaming music—just beyond the headland bordering our fields, that is what their sun is for, I almost went to see myself...And your sons are young and their blood is hot...Ai! we should do it ourselves if we knew how, friend...Our sons can see: they'll pay millions—and only last year we offered the tourists a few bunches of grapes in friendship and cursed them when they stole more the next day.

"So I sold, of course I sold!...We are almost old, you and I, we have our ways. We distrust that world, we should end the way we began, we would know where our graves will lie. Yet even we would put aside a bit if we knew how, seeing our sons run off as we weaken and finally can only drag our chairs around the square with the sun and remember the old songs. They who should take our places in the fields. Pensions, enough to keep us alive, and our sons are taken away. They hate us, they think us foolish and mean. And our wives are either with them or so cloaked in their heavy black that they see nothing. Even my oldest son, who once was like me, who knew the earth and could not leave it. He would curse the others as they left for the north and the factories, and was content to work beside me.

Two winters ago, though, you remember, he took temporary work on the yacht pier. Money came regularly, it seemed a lot. He never returned.

"Let them go, friend, let them go. Sell your lands on the sea, where the winter winds and the salt burn the plants. To keep them is to break your heart, and for no one. We are the last. Move up to the high fields where you can work in the shade of a vegetable garden. Take what grapes and olives are left each year, take your pension, send your wife into the hotels. It is enough. We are the last and the earth is indifferent."

"Sometimes I have thought that too, all of us, perhaps, our fathers too. Even this morning, as the crows circled. But then...it is only one more misery, and with our land as our only means to endure it. It will pass like the plague. Some of us will come out of it, others will have thrown themselves away."

He leans past me, I smell his sweat, to pick up a plastic pail, repaired with broad stitches of twine.

"Right does not always sit still. Who is to know? Yet...the owl's nest has fallen from the pine there and I see no signs of rebuilding."

Wild pounding: heavy boots and flailing wings. Tangle of white and tan feathers, great yellow eyes fixed calmly for an instant...silent in the roar and rush of the northwest wind...understand...startled, flapping here on the path in the bright daylight...the abandoned paths... The night is cool on the eyes, the day is cruel... Lift out of the way, soar to the edge of the brush, we shall pass in peace. Walk on, gently, for we are old friends, and the fear is the wind...once clear, fresh, singing in the pine tops, now bringing brown stinks...the sun is orange and black...farewell, go you with God...

The present is the past, the future has no meaning. I have been of the past. I have the name of heroes. We are one through the seasons, the earth, the crops, the winds, our songs, the stones of our village.

Yet my own son—I cannot be he. He has returned—his perfume smells, his unclean city voice, his fat hands. For half of a day he picked my grapes, then ate beside me at the long table on the cobblestones. Writhing and smirking to the thin sounds from his pocket radio, laughing loudly, allying with his mother against "the peasant." But I would not hide my hands, and I was silent, and the world was the thick black wine in my glass.

He will not come here, here in the dark cellar where the rats rattle among the old bottles and tomato cans, where the vaulted ceiling presses down with its curtains of dusty spider webs, where the damp earth soaks up the rotting grapes. Enough. One man's work now, with the vat half empty. And I would hardly need that candle—my hands can find their way on this ring of chestnut staves, my feet in the floating pulp.

Still, he might, looking for another flask of my wine. I could throw my hat on the candle now, from here, and if he comes with his torch I could crouch. Wine in the making will sour from a woman in heat—I would not have him here…Shadows, excuses…My father too, we have always put the candle there on the ground, with the bowl and the soap and clean towel for our feet, then climbed up into the vats with our paddles and pitchforks…Shadows, time, seeping stains on the stone, trembling in the drafts, the sucking sounds and the sweet and the grape-must…O brave Redbeard, on and away!…The shadows would disappear, the slow dancing, the empty vats, the stains of centuries. He would not know, I should not be seen.

Ashamed. Why am I ashamed?

N19
97 OT SO BAD, not so bad." That's what I tell you, no, it is not so bad, here on the *continente*. Without the elevator, though, without that we'd be long gone. Bent like this, twist my neck to even see you, look up at you. She, she's lost the fat, but the strength too—and her bite, thanks to God. Did she tell you her little joke? Lucky we are too old to make love; with our pacemakers we'd fuse each other in a short circuit.

A glass of "holy wine?" Still some left. Even a few grains of sand in the bottle from the granite ledges where we'd spread the grapes to sweeten in the sun. No, I don't go back. Can't. The boys, they come sometimes, wives, grandchildren. No outsiders till you.

Your health, your health. Yes, thank you, ages well, not like us. Color of pine sap, yes. Sweet like our wild honey.

Here, I want you to have this, this tape. She held the machine near while I sang my old songs—remember the feast days? And some new ones. Not much to do here. Songs, guitar, television . . . pasta with sauce from a tube . . . no donkeys, no bells, no need. They give us this. Rewards.

Here, I'll fix that. The scirocco, it scrapes that pine against the window, scratching like it'd come in. No, never mind? Yes, I know, and sometimes, when she's not looking—she chides still—I open the window for a bit, let the needles tickle me, smell the resin through the city fumes, listen still for the owl.

Till we meet again, comrade, till then.

A Rat in the Board Room

Dudley

FEVERISH...am I lying on my mother's bed, hot pillows, pains throbbing in my joints, her voice distant in the ringing?...slowing, dimming, gone. Confused flights, circling returning paths of the past. Identity, it slips away, forms change...

A clown dances on a circular cardboard strip under a brilliant lantern—a zoetrope, whirled by a wooden crank on wooden spokes into a squirrel-cage cog, clicking—legs flung up, spread, to kick outstretched finger tips, the pratfall to the floor, bouncing up. Over and over again while I laugh and laugh. Light reflecting on Grandpapá's shiny skin as his hand goes round and round and round, white with its strings of veins which I could pluck and rip away and leave a thin blue trickle, hands which saved my father from the wolves once on the frozen lake where the smoking ships anchor now. I shall have sons one day and I shall crank for as long as they wish and I shall laugh too for it is funny and I shall not mind about their hair...but I did brush it and brush it, yes Grandpapá...but where is it?

The bones of my fingers—fingers that once could

crank the zoetrope for my grandchildren—and the dents, the pulsing veins, dry wrinkles form and disappear, like the skim of grease on cooling soup stock, but only a thin fuzz of mildew here and there. I'm dead pale, I can see it in my mirrors.

Mirrors, I told them it was so hard to move my numb body without upsetting something, and that with mirrors about me I could see better what I was doing. These mirrors, they are my friends, they confirm me, they reassure me. Without them there's the dreadful slipping away, the ground spinning up into my face, the controls, my joystick, all loose and useless, the blinding crash—torn into fragments and each a childhood to forget. I might have thought once that when one was old—when does old begin?—one would avoid these faithful reminders of age and death (for I look like death, I have no illusions). Better that, though, than having to move and roll and rattle the bed to prove that I exist. With the interminable fussing, hands in their white uniforms pushing me about, canes, the awful fear of falling—I am thankful she is not alive, she would laugh at me, I could not bear her laughter— they drive me too hard, I am an old man, all those faces, I am too weary to try yet I am afraid of that slipping. But my eyes are still not wearied after those excursions and I can open them whenever I will and see my image—she would have said "see myself" and looked scornfully at me when I corrected her—to confirm that I am. I have too often slipped and then returned painfully, as if born anew, not to realize that my existence is all, is the only thing that is.

The church, I've channeled wealth to them, more when I finally die. They say sensible things there— Puritan origins, our New England—essential to the morality of the people. God and immortality are necessary, but of course they cannot be pressed. Those of us selected to think and know, who can deal with facts, refuse to deal personally with the future. So my mirrors reassure me. They cut short the long moments of doubt when I awake from or return from those fearful slippings and am only a flicker of awareness, a spot on the ceiling or a slight buzzing somewhere, completely detached from any brain or any part of my body. Those who really believe that God welcomes us to death, that we accept the welcome gladly, should face one of these moments. One would be enough—suspended, as it were, dead with the slimmest possibility of life. Ah! we all fight at that moment, however feeble. One single floating nerve, like a mote in the pale sun, is enough to seek a mirror, to reveal existence again. What else it reveals is incidental, however unpleasant.

Yellow-white mustache—no it's white now, wilted white, though once a glittering brown: mouse color, she said, and I guess she meant a field-mouse, her hair was city-rat gray—bushy, the nurses trim it badly. My sons wanted me to shave it off, even years ago. Old-fashioned. I suppose they thought it made the Company seem too conservative, even ridiculous—as president I should set a modern pace. Nonsense! Values last. My mustache represents respect. And she disliked it, didn't want it brushing around her, she said. So I've always kept it, ever since university. Yes, to cut it off would be a loss of my self-respect, my values (though it has changed color). Each hair is a truth—must be kept in order. My chauffeur, now, he could trim it beautifully, he could understand its value. Without my having given him the idea at all he said so right out—driving to the pier, it was, to meet my dead son's wife.

Hardly waited to bury him, my daughter said, before the woman rushes off to her foreign resorts and now that she's coming back, she'll want to sell out her stock or get a lot more out of you. You certainly should not meet her at the boat, "outrageous" my daughter said, or some such weak-minded word; outrage must be measured against rock-firm values—made the tears come to my eyes, and I was not so old then...why did my women never see my tears?

"There's a right way and a wrong way to everything. I beg your pardon sir, but it's like your mustache. She will like the flowers too. She's always spoke so well of you, sir, she has."

My neck, like a turtle's, half-withdrawn. And sometimes as I watch it, lying still, a cord will pull tight
within from my jaw to my collar bone, lifting a blood-
less membrane. Makes me fidget. Until I can forget, I
am drawn to watch for it, to try to control it.

SICKENING yellow skin on cooling breakfast
18 milk, drawn up with the edge of a table knife,
67 but I hate it, I hate it, I hate it!—to have to lift
it out and try to hide it behind my butter knife;
but blue milk runs off it and wets my butter so that I
cannot forget it, makes my stomach want to roll up
into my throat. To have to drink it, cold uncooked
chicken skin; you can't make me, I will be sick and sent
up to my room and no allowance and even the razor
strap, but you can't make me…You see, you have had
to call the doctor. Yes, Mamá, I forgive you and I feel
better, but do leave me be…I've almost finished the
"S" volume of the encyclopedia. As soon as she's gone
I can get it from the bookshelf. She'll not notice if
she comes back while I have it out. Too heavy and upsetting, she says, but that isn't true. It's so clear and
solid and useful. In four years, rather than the usual
six, I shall be going to the university…

Yes, Mamá, yes. I already have my cap and am quite
ready to go.

The sidewalks are herringbone bricks, some loose, but Mother's button shoes are used to them. A beer wagon rumbles by, two gray geldings with their shiny blinders. Mother mutters sin. A horse trolley stops to pick up a lady. As she steps up her skirt swings out showing her stockings and white frills to the others still waiting on the cobbles. More sin. Sin is a very complicated concept. I know something about it as I've just been reading that volume. But to Mamá it seems to be a collection of scenes…Her lips are so thin, like mine.

The street, from our house near the top, drops quite steeply down the hill, leveling at the bottom hyperbolically toward the river We always, from whatever direction, have to climb to go home I heard a distant relative from the south once say to Father, and there was other family in the room, that that was why we were so hard and why we saved our breath—everyone was silent in response, to prove his point, I thought.

Down we walk. The policemen wave and whistle, the iron wheels clatter, dogs and cats and a chicken or two chase about. A cow is led by, her bag veined and bursting, but I daren't look at it long or at how she winds her tail to one side and splashes a great green-brown pad almost at mother's feet; "there ought to be a…" Seagulls laugh at us, mean. Everyone is looking at me, I see smiles, hear laughs when we have gone by, boys race along the other side of the street and I'm sure they are pointing at me, though I will not look. It is always this way. My breeches are velvet and my cap is proper, but both are shabby and too tight. They laugh for my fanciness, they laugh that my clothes should be newer. I cannot escape. They only make me look straight ahead, raise my chin a bit...the Esplanade, the River, and along the far shore the University.

It is better here on the Esplanade. Quite abruptly the city stops its meanness and jangling and jeering. There are still people, of all sorts, but this is a neutral zone. Of course we don't approve of the Esplanade, the way the City runs it and rents it out. At night they kiss and hug and there are bad women and people called foreign elements. Others that are called idle, and drunken men and dirtying dogs and pencil beggars and organ grinders and carts selling old books and dusty prints. But there are also almost always some of our class—neighbors, members of our church, relatives. For we all use the Esplanade, even though it may be the long way around, from our homes to the center of the city. Fresh air and exercise. Civic responsibilities. And I like it too because it does not notice me.

I can just see City Hall standing guard, as it were, at the end, a medieval fortress, turrets and portcullis and a green grass moat, except it is all of sooty brick. And the shops of this and that beyond. My stomach sinks and the rims of my ears are hot. The antique stores are there too where she has gone with me before to search and argue about prices and origins when they know she will not buy a thing.

Perhaps we shall not go that far, though. Sometimes it is to buy a potted flower—they last longer, if your father insists that we must have something—from the carts along the riverbank. Sometimes to leave off her charity knittings or report some infraction of the moral code at the Society, which is in another fortress at the other end of the Esplanade. I never know, just: "We shall be going out in ten minutes. Prepare yourself."

It's always her heavy gray dress and black shoes and umbrella, or the coat and boots and muff in the winter. And her gloves. I am not to hold her hand when we walk, not to soil or wear out her glove. And not to be sentimental: it is up to us to show the way.

Hell used to have a turnstile, you paid admission. As fire engines set fires. And there were angels picketing it, flocking in your path, calling to you in pigeon voices not to enter. There were laughter and drink, whirling music and machines, sweets and prizes, to entice you in. The devils were women without clothes on, men on platforms yelling and waving and red-faced.

That was when I was quite young. I shouldn't tell Mother, though, she scorns childish ideas. And we are modern, we do not believe that hell is specific. Our minister hardly mentions it. I think it is a kind of eternal regret of a failure to live up to the code, a sickness from pleasure, or a shame before those who succeeded, or a dark closet of punishment forever. And heaven is the parent, the power to ignore and to be-better-than and to punish, the being right without effort, the eternal seat of honor, punctual and orderly, with stern authority reaching out in all directions to direct the proper progress of mankind.

Why is the air so clear and brilliant over the Park? Perhaps to mark the contrast better with the evil below.

I no longer play the game of Will-she-not-turn?. Foolish, even for a child, for we of course shall turn either left or right. Yet there it is before us, straight ahead, with its turnstiles clicking, its thin music noises, its sick sweet smells, its wanting-me. The Park. "Foolish is he who holds himself to be beyond the reach of evil. Do not tempt evil, do not scorn evil, do not flaunt before evil. To do so is to sin, for it justifies evil." Yet we have had relatives from distant cities, even people from other countries, who want nothing else but to see the Park and to enter it. Impatient to get pasted to their luggage the blue triangles saying "The Park City" as if that were all we were and all we had.

Stands of postcards, racks and racks of them. I know better now than to look at them: the Ferris wheel in the center with young ladies waving their hats, wanton, the green esplanade with City Hall at one end and Society at the other, the river with its rowers, the distant twisted towers and bulbous spires of the University; the ladies in a line on the stage throwing high their skirts to leer with their drawered bottoms; the kiss behind the parasol; the paintings of naked men and women from our museum; the boat races, the bathers, the sunset behind our skyline.

We turn toward the Society, passing the fences and hedges which close off the Park. A gust of wind coming from the river brings the smell of the tidal mud below the wall of the Esplanade—the stale smell of an unaired washcloth. And now the starch and soap of Mother's dress, acid urinal stinks under the walls of the Society, the sweeter horse manure, the dust of autumn leaves burning in my lungs. I myself have no smell, or perhaps no-smell is a smell like no-color is black. She says we cannot smell ourselves and should therefore wash well regardless, yet she must be wrong for often I can smell myself, just as if I were someone else. Not now, though. I am perfectly neutral; like a solution I change drop by drop until the litmus hangs purple between the blue and the pink. It's pleasant like this—removed, observing everything, untouchable. Here on the Esplanade, people, Mamá too, are suspended in their thoughts and their errands, not looking for others. So I am unseen too. There is no need to tolerate them. Power through morality, knowledge, production...black fortress walls, black with soot...a waste, a leaf whirling on the walk...control the wind, turn pleasure into progress. Nothing will sap me, reason will climb higher and higher until the whole plan can be deduced and then ordered...it is splendid to be good and to be right...Litter Here...do not, do not, do not...correct, one hundred percent, checkmate.

Cries from the top of the Ferris wheel. Gas lights flare against the beet-red sky. The chill of the autumn night will drive them away. Brisk walking is the way to warm the blood, feed the brain.

I **1957** FEEL MY BLOOD, waves, slow tides...the gravity of my heart. I am old, very old...the momentum of the nearly perfect pendulum, silken cord, polished steel ball, airless chamber, set swinging, swinging on in its own plane without regard to the turning of the world, dying from the friction of a thread, a few molecules of gas. Determination becomes habit. And once I was a boy walking the Esplanade with his Mamá. Yes, if I wished I believe that I could remember. But I must beware, I must continue the careful checking for life—habits can lie too long. The feeble steps, the mirrors, the unfamiliar faces. I need these to tell me that I am not lost forever in other lives. Even now, with this resolve, I know that I have slipped often. Waking from sleep is distinct—the slow creep of wakefulness along my nerves and muscles, the languor, the stiffnesses, the steep gathering to focus, the rheums which clog and stink in my cavities. But these other returns—a sudden awareness, a projected image on a screen flicked off and all rustling darkness about uncomfortable identity, the nearness of death and the distance of life. Bittersweet...confounded song! From sleep one wakes or dies, from...But what? How can I tell what? It is only the negative side of this awareness, this knowing that I am here, old, very old.

This crumpled cheek. How many thousands of times have I returned to it, grasped it with my eyes like an award for merit...flesh, a scrotum, a wrinkled dug— no no! Kisses of honor, the ribbon in my lapel. Worthy sons and daughters, dutiful, reaching on tiptoe, bending low over me now, flushed expected pecks from the promised wife—soon ended, that, in mutual distaste. Grandchildren, great-grandchildren—a parade, obeying the "give me a kiss, dear." Cold dry bodies, hardened, recoiling. Of course, I do not mind. Of course, otherwise the flesh. Respect to the founder, the president, the chairman, the man of science and of industry. How many have seen themselves, with their living eyes, honored on a postage stamp? Birthday greetings from kings. Biographies, magazine covers, a dictionary word for a lightbulb-sealing process. Limousines, private elevators, the only key to the private toilet, five nurses. An empire, benevolent, bringing light around the world—for their own good. A Society of stern fiber and will, enforcing right and good.

OOD MORNING, gentlemen." I am glad to see that they are all here this morning. The sun shines in obediently, the varnished cedar walls glow, they sit respectfully. The minute hand jumps to nine-o-one—that is their margin. Good men. Firm hand...Pencils, pads of paper. The stage is set. "May God bless us, bless the fruitful outcome of this meeting." The minutes: the shriving of the corporate soul, an eye on the method and rules, an eye on the desired result—Company or Society. But Company now: today's business. "Members of the Board, the Chair has before it a group of important proposals. Before considering them seriatim...a few words...principles...of all time...never to lose sight of the philosophy of our company..."

A brown photograph of a plant-opening, framed, blessed, brass plaque. Kings, presidents...my mustache dark and commanding...The air is clear. A boat whistles in the river mouth. Only the two foreign directors doodle. Ash trays—the outsized bases of our largest bulbs—never used in my presence. Aired well this morning, aided by a purifying northwest wind. They had surely expected this, but would outvote me. The voice vote, I control. "Our job is to produce, our sacred purpose. More, better, cheaper. We have climbed hard and far. We are at the top of the world industry. But we cannot stop where we are...violate our trust, the faith of our stockholders...like a mountaineer: advance or retreat...and it's in advance that the achievements of mankind are made...if government tries to block them we shall challenge them...petty socialists, mediocrities who have no understanding...the strength of our system...no secrets, no deals...know-how, excellence, chosen to lead..."

They know what's coming, even are eager for it, once they have expressed their latest theories. A strong hand, a steady goal. The ethic of our system, clear, precise as a mathematical law...reason, honesty and truth above all...the job well done.

"I understand your proposals to mean, if allowed to continue in the direction they head, restriction of markets, agreements on prices with our competitors, and no further expansion. And if anyone suggests again that we shorten the life of our filaments without passing on a more than offsetting benefit to the customer, I shall have to ask him to resign...ethics...duty to society...I shall have coffee brought in now for those who indulge, before the Chair calls for discussion." Where the effects are not serious I do make concessions to the customs of the times: coffee, but not tobacco.

And still the walls glow confidently...I was right to permit no conversation with the Chairman during these intervals. Gives me time to appraise. Still, to know, to be sure, to be right, those are the greatest teachings of our system and of our society. Good men, these, yet will any of them ever know the great men of our society, men of science, of power, of industry, of government?...But why a new water cooler? Chlorinated water for the sake of a foot pedal, bitter cold, bad for the digestion—Wild Mountain Spring serves us well, the great green bottles twice a week, soft, in paper cups— wasteful though...the years when each had his own glass, towel, soap, washroom key; bottom drawer on the right where everyone but me would prop his feet.

The vote. Motion to combine and table. "Those in favor." Not to look up, my fingers tap lightly on Parliamentary Procedure. Yeas: here and there, a few, I know, I need not look. "Opposed." Not to hear. Nays: presumably the rest, but cut short the echo. "The yeas have it." Look up slowly. All eyes are down. The minutes rapidly confirm.

*   *   *

THE CRUMPLED CHEEK. Hardly a tremor, suspended above the bedpan. Give me a kiss, my dear. Honors, yes, great honors, success, but…give me a kiss my dear, whoever you are. My daughter, daughter-in-law, my son's wife; but he?…I have only one son, yes, but this one's dead? Ah! pretty girl, pretty girl…but she has gone, you are a nurse, she is gone and she will think I did not know her. Wrinkled, crumpled mind. I would not hurt her. Will she come back? From across the ocean? But there are many oceans, how much to cross!

19 57

"Did you hear me, sir? Did you understand? That was his wife, your oldest son's. He died thirty years ago. Do answer me, sir."

"But I did, I did. No? Ah! I thought I had spoken. Yes, I understand. But did she kiss me?"

Lipstick on my crumpled cheek, perfumes. The breath of her sun-sweet Mediterranean wine, the "holy wine" she brought me once. I forbid. But I cannot and she has gone and perhaps she had forgotten, a long time, a long way. And perhaps she has more courage than the rest. Or heart…Pretty girl, why did you go away? You must not go away, leave him lying smooth gray marble beside his mother, take his daughter away! Appearances and family and honor and order. My dear, you must stay here, where we can bring the child up properly as he would have wanted…Cables and answers and then no answers, we shall not talk of her now...No, there is no slack, the code is tight, you are quite right. Still, still...

W*E ARE PLEASED* that you have come back, my dear, though no doubt we do not show it. We are not given to showing much pleasure. I regret that you did not bring the girl with you. She is my grand-daughter, you know. I should have liked to have seen her." Empty bedrooms, servants, a young girl—awkward.

"She is my daughter. I chose and there is no un-choosing. But will you take me for a walk along the river, Papá?" I am never asked, never. I walk alone, everyone knows I walk alone. Doesn't she know? And sometimes the urchins follow me, the same urchins, they never grow up. I walk to arrive, not to walk and because I am expected to. A strange lady, beautiful perhaps, bending, eluding, unanswering. My own children, I white, they gray and closed and right...In full flower —a rather distasteful term, suggestive...the Society.

"It would be a pleasure, my dear. I am quite prepared."

They would say that she is flattering me to get something from me, they with their silences and impatiences. And I suppose that they would be right. Still, I am curious, interested in this woman chosen by my oldest son, or in her who chose him, for that matter, with his deformed speech, his detachment from things immediately at hand, his position in the Society. Not much money then, either, with my empire only a vision. What would she know of that? There was position and tradition. Or was it an attraction, a weakness?

The colors of her clothing and of her features are a shade brighter than the customs of our northern city, for all its Park and its seafront and its City Hall, the flesh within more generous...shameful thoughts.

Why would she wish to walk with me?

"One needs air and motion about one's thoughts, don't you think Papá? Is not that why you walk so much and are so successful? May I hold your arm? It gives me more confidence and this walking makes me a little giddy."

"Certainly, my dear." Stiff rough wool, a gloved hand that looks like face powder gathered together. Will it dust off?...Embarrassment, the church aisle, matrimony mater mother-making, and once Mamá clinging for no more than support on the way to her grave.

"Papá, you think badly of me, all of you. No, I know it is so. He died in my arms, not in your white enamel hospital. He was incurable. They, all of you, worked on me. Years ago, yet I remember every look and word. Ah! your disapprovals, like the creeping Ice

Age. How could I but run in terror with my dying baby? To warmer places, where I was brought up. How could I have belonged here? No more could I even now —where a woman's hand on a man's arm is awkward and thoughts are all angles and high walls and metal and light bulbs. Where to sip even our *vin santo*, sun-sweetened 'holy' wines, our blood of Christ, is a sin.

"But, no no, I sound critical and I am not. Only different. There are wonderful things that are done here, upright industrious people, high standards, church-going, and your great factories, your Society doing so much good. You are so sure. Everything is explained and clear and admirable. Predictable. Your son and your daughter will carry on. The best possible foundations for your empire and for your family."

Misguided, impossible upbringing, parents always living abroad—mercifully dead now. Intelligent though, and strong-willed and not indifferent to merit and moral fiber. With time…he chose well, perhaps. She should have no more to say now that she has apologized. Tea at the women's section of the Club, though I suppose she would prefer something alcoholic. Confidence, I was upset for a moment. That awkward hand.

"Only different, Papá. Other gods, other codes, other hearts. There are many others. For me, here, there is missing the state of grace, and without grace about me, recognizable somewhere within reach of my faint heart, I feel hollow, empty, I forget how to smile. For me morality has no meaning without grace lying beyond it, all about it. But I am hopeless at explaining. You see, nothing stays still, I think, and yet morality would have it do so...Forgiveness is full understanding, not just accepting apologies."

Feeling without mind, it will never do. Is this criticism? Decadent, soft, and to try to strike at us with such softness, us with our determination, at us who are right.

"How gay your Park is, how delightful, here in the somber north! Yet none of you have been inside? How sad...But I have said too much, I don't mean to anger you...Papá, will you give your granddaughter a puppy? I should take it back with me. Puppies are worth all the money and production and progress in the world. Do! That is why I asked you to take me for a walk, to find the courage to ask. Does it sound silly? I fear it does, I see it does from your face...But she cannot remember you and perhaps will never see you again. We were waiting for you when you crossed the ocean to receive your decoration. But of course, you were far too busy...'Yes, he was my grandfather and he gave me a puppy when I was a little girl...' But I could not bear deception. It is only that I wanted you to know what sort of girl she is—so that you might know, if you chose, how to remember her."

THERE, there is no more. Many times she has come to take me for that walk. Once I *19 57* asked her for a kiss, and I think she gave it to me, lightly on the cheek... Did she kiss me, did she?...Please, do not argue with me, I am tired and quite old, you shouldn't argue with an old man. Send her a puppy, nurse, my granddaughter who is abroad, a spitz, I think, it is the only one I know, and quickly, time and we may have missed...but no, it doesn't matter, her age. I know it is what she wants and will remember. The others have never asked, but she, but she...Who am I then, do I not control, is this not my bed, my mirror, window, house, city? Do you not understand?...Of course I do not wish to sleep, my nap is over. And why are you here, where is my mother? I am to go with her this afternoon, I must not be late. Leave me be, horrid, horrid, I will beat you, you must not touch me, shame!

Shifting, sliding, lighter from darker across lighter ...longer, shorter, counterflows crossing, passing on and out...ghosts before the end, draining away, fading into eternal shadows... Faint rumblings, clatterings, punctuation, thundering scratchings... Flappings of sound and light, separate, together, connection. Change gives time, progression. Denser, thicker.

Then losing, going, lesser to lesser to limitless unending end...

Slight, dim, soft…finest dusting of light on dark, silentest sound of sound. Return, repeat, remember. Shifting, sliding, lighter, darker—rumblings, clatterings. Remote—weaving patterns relating light and sound— accumulating. Alien, yet enwrapping. Without identity but encompassing all, admitting no observation, no apartness, no other time or space, no other existence—suspension in death.

A quickening, a massing stronger, faster, heavier. Sound broken into swelling rushing bits, images hurtling through each other, pressing, pressed. Entering me. I. Death, death's subject.

There's the chance! Would there be an I in death? The alien sensations rush in on me still. Am I opposed to them or part of them? Could there be such a question in death? Or any question? Test it: But there is no sensation of existence, no body to contain soul. Nothing but the flashing images and the roar occupying all, no receiving, no recording, no motion, no materiality, no independence. But there is memory or I should not seek undeath, desperately, as I do. In despair, in terror of this suspension, between explosion and shrinking to nothing.

The images are drifting aside. They no longer fill all space. In halting steps and jerks they retreat. They are replaced. By a suffusion, by lines, by color, by whiteness. By a hand. Mottled brown on green-yellow, sucked dry, shining—a splendid hand, an old man's hand. Once I thought for a dreadful time that it was a great spider, hairy, splotched venomous markings, perched horridly on top of folds and forms of white expanse. It seemed to clutch its prey under it, slowly turning it in its jealous legs, relishing the weak struggling.

But my mirror tells me. It is a hand, all right, my hand, resting, storing its energies on the edge of the bed. How many things it has done! How many honors it has won and accepted, temptations rejected! A few shames hidden. Until recently I have thought of it as only part of me, or perhaps I have not really thought of it at all. Yet, though it has been a close companion, it has its own memories and its own life, and often it has had more vigor and wisdom than I. How often it has found the winning chess moves or reached out to slap order and decision, or found just the right pressures for the ranks of hands on factory rounds, or stepping down from the podia.

N_{18}^{67}O, CHILD! You must not put your hand there. I can tell even without pulling back the sheets. It is nasty and dirty. Evil. Leave yourself alone. If I catch you again I shall have to tell your mother." I was sleeping. Cool sheets tight like a bowstring to the curving mattress. Cool my burning cheek. My heart beats in my pajama pocket—shame, temptation, damnation, a wickedness aching in me. But I shall conquer it, I am to be great.

Waxed wood floors, black and glowing from the street lights, they're cold on my bare feet. I can just hear a voice and rustling and silence from the living room below, make out faint outlines of the banister, the gas turned low on the landing. I have so many facts and things in my head and I must get them into order before I sleep, walking here, up and down the long hall, where I settle things...They jeer at me, but I am not ashamed. Their insults merely tighten me, my fists. I am small and they point at me in the showers. It does not matter. I will show them! Those downstairs there too, they do not understand. They think I am a child, a little boy, but I am strong, resistant. Yes, I shall show everyone! Look temptations in the eye. They will see, they will see.

Here's the window now, hidden at the end of the crooked hall. That's why Mother has never put curtains on it though she should, for the air drops down cold in front of it into a pool emptying in a slow stream along the wainscot. I have waded in the stream, on winter nights, right to the edge where it drops into the stairwell through the weir of the banister. Squatting on the blanket chest, in the faint cedar smell, hugging my knees tight under my chin, my thighs pressing against me, clutched hard—I hold off the cold, the trembling deep fevers. Not to look out the window, not until I have contained my warmth, prepared, controlled. Then...

The sky beyond the outlines of the rooftops and chimneys is a feeble yellow glow, dirty, a dull outline. The chimneys are squat and square, nothing for storks or witches or the rest, solid and practical, modest, none of the competing shapes and angles, elbows and hats, that I have seen in pictures. The windows, it is early still, many are lighted behind their shades and curtains. And the waves of dimness spread out over the city in their complicated patterns, ebbing and flooding: hydraulics, pressures and flows and resistances, of the city gas system. Soon they will turn down the street lights below me; it is only a backstreet with no through traffic on it. Reflections in a thousand squares, like graph paper, on the cobblestones wetted in streaks by the horses. Ammonia, and the moist mushroom smell of the droppings—just beyond this thin black glass, molecules thickly floating over the city. The bitter yellow smell of coal smoke. Cedar and dust and silver polish and cold mahogany, laundry bleach and bluing, on my side of the glass, and a few molecules of dead decaying rat.

Even these molecules cannot move through the glass. I certainly don't. It's not the way poets would have it. I quite know where I am, and I am neither closed in nor closed out. Facts matter, position, object related to object, not to some passing viewpoint. I am here. And I'm not wrapped in molecules, they just happen to be here too. Beyond the glass are more but different molecules, some of them arranged in objects, some in smells. Some seek others and burn together, compose and decompose.

Women in the windows waiting, men seeking the door, coming and going, shades lowered and raised. I know about it. It is called a brothel, or more usually "that house." I am to know nothing of it, as if it would corrupt me or harm me in some way. Quite the contrary, I am strengthened by observing and understanding these weaknesses. It is obviously the adults who are corruptible, not I—with their abuses of their God-given powers, their degradations of womanhood and manhood. Sitting here, watching, studying, I have learned control over the pains and fevers and ugly temptings, I have learned of an evil that must be stamped out, crushed, and I shall find the power to do it.

Faint sounds of copper toes and iron shoes and wooden wheels on the cobblestones click against the window glass. The house breathes around me in blacks and browns, yellows, dimly. The waves of hot dry breath from the furnace grates rise along my spine, shivering on my neck, fall coldly down the glass, drawing me in tightly. Laughter, maybe, through their glass and the splotched orange shades pulled up from the sills halfway. Or snarls and cries from the hunger and fear on their faces, the haste and the wrestling on the bed, through the single pane of the upper sash pulled open a crack. Molecules escaping, they shall not enter here. Lights swinging, circling, fading, sharpening, hard and cutting. A door opens, closes, opens, yielding, casting out. Resisting, exorcising, held at bay, cowering. My pride against them, the ache of pride, the weight and steel and flash of pride...No, no, no! I shall crush you. Retreat! Whores, vile men! Wait for me, you will hear me. Vile, filthy...A wall of scarlet flecked with orange rises before me, a scorched wind roars. Silence is fixed, suspended in a white flame. Released, dissolving, unclenching, receding.

COOL AIR, cool sheets towards the edges, a fumbling from the direction of the door.

1957   "He was no more than thirteen when they moved from there. I remember hearing of that house in back from someone. Extraordinary. Each month he slips further back in time. Death would be merciful. He is no longer Papá. His eyes seem empty of everything around him."

Who is this they would have dead? Some old man.

I cannot tell from their whisperings. Grownups are so devious.

I AM ILL. I am not going to the birthday party. They have tricked me and are taking me instead to the hospital? My hands are cold and yellow, spotted with brown. I must wash them when I arrive. Ugly, crusted, I shall hide them under the carriage rug, carefully hold them away not to soil my party suit. And why do they tremble?

Why is everything so quiet, and we go so fast? There's a faint hum, like the tea-time kettle. Are those trumpets sounding in the distance? And these sudden stops and starts. No horses, no trees, no sky, no sun. The windows are swollen and stretched. Everything outside is straight lines and angles, and the lights—greens and reds and violets—winding and looping like spaghetti. Blackness, flashes that ache in my eyes. Bad gas smells — I must tell a grownup, it is dangerous. Do you hear me, don't you smell it? You'll poison us or blow us up.

Where are the curtains? And outside are layers and layers of windows in walls that rise to the sky, but no houses. Somehow seeming to wrap around me is the sick-sweet heavy music that we heard, was it yesterday?, from the bandstand, with cookies and cambric tea. But where is the band, I see no band, they sound right here, but where are they?

Why don't you answer me, why don't you listen to me? Are you not my parents, fur and wool and gloves? Of course you are, but I must not look up or you will see how ill I am. And I must not speak again or you will know how my eyes whirl and how everything has turned strange, how frightened I am.

There is a bug crawling across the carriage window— it is the same, it is my friend! Look! Do you see him? Do look, he hasn't changed a bit, and I believe he knows me. Crawling across the face of layers and layers of windows without curtains, of giant-children's blocks stacked up in order to trap all these shiny buzzing wingless flies. He doesn't care a bit for all that, with his double tail like a lemon fork...no, you may not, it would curdle the milk. Twenty-five, twenty-two, twenty-three—but it must be even...legs, wiggling like a worm, but fast. Hungry, his long tongue sweeping back and forth on the glass collecting sticky sweet globs of invisible food, looping back under his chin to pull it through his mouth as I do a spun-sugar stick...A horrid boy, and I was six a long time ago. Will they have spun sugar?...His legs move in waves like the teeth of my comb when I run my finger along them. I shall stay like this, leaned forward close to him, so they will not see him. They would call him something awful and would crush him with a newspaper so that he would squirt out his life like paste...Like this. A tiny struggle under my thumb, it makes me shiver. Dry and crispy like a scab. He flattens, smudging yellow, bits of lemon...Rubbing my thumb fast back and forth on the plush, it burns.

"Could you reach the chauffeur's panel? It's an important step we're considering. You should know about it...one of the major stockholders, his daughter."

"It's closed. What is it? Does it matter that Papá's here?"

"How could it? He doesn't even recognize us anymore; he is in a world that no longer is. We are preparing to change the name of the Company, drop his name which is so old-fashioned. We'll prepare the papers—he'll sign anything and we can get reliable witnesses."

"I shan't object. And it's no use thinking of him as alive now. A vegetable. Look at him. It would have been so much better for him, for everyone, if he had died many years ago."

D AYDREAMING, I have little else, though at times it is painful and confusing. As I am, I am intolerable, even to myself. Perhaps they should take away the mirrors. What difference, what possible difference could it make? There is no need for reflections. I have accumulated everything worthwhile—so old, old as experience, and satisfied, replete. There is no need to die or to live, only to continue, nourished by what I know, protected by my rewards. An existence which needs no confirmation from mirrors, an existence no one could know until age comes to shut off all necessity except the self.

I daydream within my self. I return, I remember, I construct even. But it is never quite complete, perhaps if it were that would be death. As it is, there's a superimposing—ghosts threaten, while I would grasp only for something whole, complete, uninterrupted. I fight off the ghosts, trying to close them out, to distract them, or to reinforce the surrounding so that the haunting pales away to nothing—but I never succeed for long.

Active to the end, as if it were admirable. I pity them. Yet my obituary reads—how many times have I read it!—active in affairs until the age of ninety-five. Not too bad, even if he didn't quite make it. And after ninety-five? Intolerable, he should have died.

No, no, then began the turning inward. I no longer try to explain it to them, there is no need, and they will not listen. They think me quite out of reach, no longer of their species at all, because this is the way they want to think of me. I do not obstruct them. I lack the will but also the interest. It is no longer important.

No, the ghosts will not go away. Scenes behind scenes, sounds behind sounds. His memory is gone, I hear them say—it is not true. I store away everything. It is that I use it differently now and do not care about the others. I still have the chess games, every one of them, each move, each opponent, and the Company statistics, annual production, every balance sheet item for seventy-five years. But I have no time now to bother with it, my time is so large. I seek to understand details. I am no longer building up facts, using my memory for that, constructing goals and principles. Instead I wander softly, slowly, disturbing no one, through minutiae, finding in them a lightness, and interest, a fascination (a word I would have turned away from before) which is quite new to me. Perhaps this is delight. Would I ever have thought that I should know delight, occupy all my great age in it? Delectation? It could never be explained to them, how could it? No, I am right to close out everything current. It is only when I look into one of my mirrors for a long time, studying myself, looking for the detail in my eyes, that I can see my mask of blankness, my empty eyes, as they say, gradually become transparent, revealing my private interest.

Now, it is happening now—I shall keep the mirrors—as I lie on pillows and stare into this mirror close beside me. My eyes are filling, deepening, I can see my life within. But this is not a reward, I was wrong. It is not a question of deserving, these few half-gained delights. It is a gift, a reprieve from a life that would have shut them out for myself and for everyone. For my children. There I succeeded too well, from what I see of them. I do observe them, study them, and I see my success. There is no changing things. So I am empty before them, I do not try to meet them. Perhaps, though, they will be granted a reprieve too, but it will not be my doing. Each must work it out. Enough of cases and principles. They led me far from appreciation. I have nothing to say to others. No one can heed or learn this, expect or find this. It is a pure gift.

No, my reward is the ghosts, the thick translucencies, the incubi of my dreams. Demons. Ghosts behind ghosts, uninvited voices, wishing my power, my resignation, my wealth, my name, my honor, my death. Even my death—a costly nuisance—and they are right, by the principles they have learned from me. They cannot know that I have been given back my life...You could merely stop the injections, his lungs would fill up, and that would be the end of this misery...*This* misery, they said, not *his*—nor was I in misery except from hearing them, my children—who actually had no care of me. Something saved me then, perhaps the power of the gift. But will it again?

Strange, my eyes are filled with tears. Not just the

wateriness which flattens old eyes, but flowing streaking tears, tears flooding the folds of my decaying face. They see too much, for they have been there before. The simple, dignified ceremony, family, a few close friends; we welcome gifts to the Society, no flowers please. The hired gray gloves, the hurrying murmurs, the afternoon sun pale through the lead glass. The children, old themselves, looking backwards to be sure the rules are followed, one resenting the other (which one? it does not matter) who had too clearly told the papers "close friends" and inexcusably given the governors and presidents and seats of power their excuse to stay away. The grandchildren have come, though, many from far away, for this last duty to the bequests. The office staff is arranged by salary, and the few remaining colleagues from the Society. The new minister, who has learned not to pray and not to look things in the eye, gladhands about. No coffin, I am not there. And there is no need to turn on the lights.

We're up there now, on that knoll where I put her and our oldest son under their polished stones. Beside them, waiting. Hermetic glove-gray coffin hidden beneath pine branches not to offend the last visitors. The grass is clipped, turning brown for the winter, the trees are forever green, uninterested. The roar of traffic increases, from all sides, the ground trembles and is never to be still. The lights will be coming on now, never to be dark. The black limousines wind up the driveway. Only family and the minister are there, standing about awkwardly, one or two coming over to read the inscriptions. The light is blue in the exhaust and the cold autumn mists. They eye their watches, the traffic mounts. They purr warmly away.

There are to be no tears, no heart. The hands of the nurses that have cared for me, perhaps they will tremble on wet cheeks, but they are of another land, born under another sun, and have not been conditioned enough yet by us. Or only that these gentle rough women did not know me before.

There is to be no last look, folded hands resting by the ribbons and the rosette, eyelids drawn from wasted hollows smoothly over the eyes that held much, lips at rest. No cold kisses, no watching through the night. No bearers, no volleys or salutes, no shot or bugle for the hero, no speech for the honored, for the powerful, for the achiever. No splendor. No last farewell.

He should have died, he should have died. There is no one left...Ah! Finally. What a relief. It is better so. I am glad for your sake. Certainly for the best.

Where has she gone? Did she kiss me? Will she come for my funeral? She would know me now, she would understand, if only she would stay and I could talk to her. They have told her I am old and wandering, she will not come again. She will be too far away to return when the telegram arrives. And she will say to herself that this was her last farewell. Did she kiss me? Why can I not remember? I should pay with everything I have to know, yet they have taken from me even the power to pay. No power but to look into my mirrors and into my heart, to learn to distinguish life from death. No hope but to await the tears of these women who drift about me, who smile, who care for me.

Other faces pass, smileless, angled and askew. Distorted, wavy, as through flowing tears. Bodiless faces, and they are so impossibly distant, though quite large, beyond all reach, all infinite effort. Or are they illusion, nothing there to be reached, only posing appearances disguising space? Busy, concerned with pressing affairs, impatient with the present, hurrying on importantly. My faces. They turn away and disappear. And others enter. They waver less, seem closer, substantial in the unbordered diffused light. If I were to reach out, though, they would avoid me, uncertain of the meaning, hesitant and worried and weakened. Yet I can see their hands too, and they are strong and accurate, though dull like disused tools. Somehow the faces themselves seem disused, left behind and abandoned. And though they try, turning here and there, searching, sometimes looking right at me, they, like the first faces, are unable to see me. Gradually they disperse, wandering away until there are none.

And other forms appear. This time they are complete, face and limbs and body, form, resisting space. Their arms are crossed, their legs fixed to the ground. They stand about me quietly, looking at me, seeing me, and sometimes smiling in recognition. There is no disguise in their eyes or fear or impatience, but they are heavy with sorrow. Their bodies are strong, efficient, necessary, not alien and disused. By the way they remain still, the way their clothes reveal muscle and bone, by the calmness of their eye and the smell of earth, I know them. Take me back, I would have you take me back! I beg you! It is a long way, I know, but have I not already set out on the path?

Lowell, Dudley's son

SOMETHING of danger, something beyond my control, has awakened me. It has happened to me before, in the wilderness, these long moments to recapture the particular sound that shattered my sleep. The brook runs on, louder though, it had grown distant as I watched the stars through the tent flap, as I pleased myself with my efficiency at camp-making, as I forgave her her clumsinesses and her headaches, as my muscles slowly turned to sleep.

I hear an echo. Sharp from the cliffs beyond a far scream begins. Instantly from within my head I hear the original, a dreadful scream of death reaching out to all life, freezing every heart. And a struggling and flapping, and stillness.

She is awake for I hear her breath released. "My God! What was that?" She can hardly whisper it.

"Nothing. Why do you have to wake me? Just some rabbit being taken by an owl." Why does she never know the answers? Forever I'm pulling her along.

Nature is a set of knowable facts. I exercise my brain and my body on them. With application one can outreach the specialists..."You would make a good peasant"—Papá (Dudley, name's extinct) with his superior look...or mathematician, or explorer, or statesman, or naturalist, or financier, or...but I am a manufacturer—production, the greatest benefit to the most, expansion, progress, better for less so more can appreciate more. Happiness. Papá wouldn't admit to happiness, but that's it: so more can be happier, leisure, comfort, health, security. And I am here to use my body and brain differently for a few days, replenishing, and to show the others I can beat them nevertheless. Papá, he hides away in his chess games—I could beat him too if I played half as much as he—hiding from new products and market agreements and the politics of modern business, with his "When I was a boy..." and his bankrupt Society, his outmoded measures, his hanging on to the top long after his time. He decries my recreations and my knowledge of the natural world.

But I don't understand him. How could he say "Perhaps we killed..."? That certainly was not my reason for suggesting to the Board a high pension for the widow. He was a valuable man to us, he was my friend... became unbalanced...suicide. That is all. That is enough. But "We killed him," ridiculous!

I mourn him. Another's weakness strengthens one, but to see him breaking...I was with him a great deal in these last years—working together. New factories, the legislature...Perhaps there were hints, but what could I do? Even to the end he was usually sound, brilliant. Quicker than anyone I have known. Yet he would veer, shy off without reason, worry a point with too much reason. The doctors say these were signs...And he worshipped her, called her inconceivably pure—to my face, nothing wrong with it. She, lying here, snoring a bit. Unconscious, unassailable purity. Perhaps that's what he always wanted but could never have, and so he could only die.

But that is too romantic. No, he was practical too, sound, a first-rate engineer. But he could lose his way in a maze of principles and conflicts. Public interests, private interests, restraints of trade, duty to stockholders, tax avoidance. He saw compromise as immoral, as violating integrity, yet he was unable to choose.

And once...We had visited a factory, a new complex, almost desert land, everything from the ground up, houses, a school, shops, cinema, sports fields. And the factory itself was humming. We had watched from the control tower, men in the new orange uniforms moving expertly about making the small adjustments, experimenting here and there. Our plant manager had showed us around, giving orders in asides—capable man, no nonsense of rank or the old-fashioned effort to please.

We were back at the hotel, in the bar, after the usual party for "head office" to meet "field." He began to talk, but as if to himself. I, certainly his closest friend then, was quite left out. How did he begin? I had been trying to lay out the factors involved in deciding whether or not to go ahead with a new unit at this factory, trying to get him to check and add to my analysis. But he would not respond. He had an air of isolation, as if removed behind a vacuum, though he was looking straight into my eyes and seemed to be understanding what I was saying. Cost factors, political climate, new markets, competition—and then I talked, excitedly, of the philosophy of business expansion. That was what started him—he must have been taking in what I was saying. He interrupted me, stopped me abruptly, with a violent gesture. His hand, which had been lying still on the table by his untouched glass— the whisky lay in a distinct oily layer below the water and ice, that annoyed me somehow—his hand suddenly stiffened, the fingers stretched out, bent back at the knuckles to their limit, lifted slightly from the table. I stopped, not because this gesture was a signal in conversation, but from a feeling that something had happened to him, that I was no longer in his presence. It was a gesture entirely to himself.

"Where? Where does this lead? Why am I on this course? What is this to me? It is folly. The Desert Flower! We the propagating bees. The age of reason, begot by the age of enlightenment. We shall inherit...destiny

…man the tamer of raw nature…complacent, sure, chosen, God in his image…Is there no enough, no satisfaction, no peace, always more, never less? All ends, nothing ends. But we have finally destroyed the cycling forever. The wheel has flown apart and the rim stretches out in fatal trajectory…It is insane, yet I know nothing else; there is only one end, one escape."

She and I, we don't talk much to each other, except sentimentalities at the appointed times. And it is late, my eyelids twitch with fatigue, my elbow aches from a tensed nerve, my head is buzzing and running down, alcohol mostly burned out. I know the pattern after ten years of it. Get home in silence, that's my usual goal, for I feel her to be alien and critical and I do not want to be told. Of course I am right and she would come to agree, but I'd rather not have to make the effort.

The letter to the president of our biggest customer—the most powerful company in the world, no doubt of it—regretting that I could not join him and his son on a hunting trip. She heard me talking about it. "But I would send a copy back to the boys at the office and they would be even more impressed by a refusal than an acceptance. And when I thought of this I didn't mind that I couldn't make it. We have first-class people, but they just don't know the really important men of the world." I am guilty of something, I can feel it from her. So I would rather silence. It is enough to run the Company and make Papá a wealthy man without having to justify it to her.

But she begins, stirring, looking out the window, hunching down into her coat. "I wish...that word important...I know what you say, but it is so...You really shouldn't tell that story. If others feel the way I do, you..."

"But I was joking. And you saw the way they understood it, laughing and agreeing and talking about dirty-work and window-dressing. You just don't understand. And besides, you must admit"—I am being very understanding in the circumstances—"that one must always have some criterion based on importance. If it's not on power in the business world then it will be on something else: the size of the symphony orchestra he conducts, or the number of votes, or his bibliography, or the quickness of his muscle, or the merit of his good works. And isn't it...wouldn't it be hypocritical to scorn the very criterion on which the modern world is based and which has brought us our happiness and comforts?" There, I feel better. I was quite right.

I say my prayers, silently, lying in the cold dark to the distant city roar, the owl in our oak tree, her steady breathing across the room. Every night, I have never failed that I remember, though it is not something I would talk about. Even she does not know. But it reassures me, that I am right, that I am in relationship with the great design, and helps me reconsider abstractly. And I do believe in God. I can think of no one I admire who is an atheist.

Before me is a great portal studded with iron spikes. I must tip my head far back to look up its height. Slowly it opens in halves, rumbling rollers on quarter-circle tracks, by its own will and impulsion. I step forward confidently on the worn stone floor. The next door is an unframed sheet of glass which opens with a sigh when I step on the treadle. Much like my office outer door. A blank smooth wall of wood paneling is in front of me. With a whirring, an entire section, where I had seen no seams before, slides aside, moved from within. I enter calmly, controlling my inner excitement—for an instant I remember a ceremony at which I was awarded a high honor: the multitudes of envious or indulgent faces, the strange floating sensation of the brain when limbs and motion are forgotten.

How can I have the detachment to be watching myself as from some unknown dimension at this crucial moment? I can observe my excitement. I am me, and at the same time I am the enormous dark space behind that panel enclosing me. It is some privilege which I must accept without understanding.

Two lines of white figures stretch out before me on either side. From huge forms nearby they diminish into the distance until they are lost in an empty point. Dimly in the black behind each row I can see a line of polished columns——somehow I know that they are stainless steel. Beyond them, immensely far and certainly not to be seen, I sense the final walls, perhaps by the faint echoing of my footsteps. The columns extend high into the darkness, somewhere in the gloom there is a ceiling. I can feel its weight lifting my shoulders as if to give me wings. The floor is of glass, faintly glowing. I have the feeling of being watched from below, hiding in the shadows of my cheekbones.

I am not surprised by this vast lustered hall behind the portal and façade of the ancient temple. I have expected it. But I am increasingly excited. And now I become aware of another foreseen element: the combination of faint odors that hang unchanging in the still warm air. There are the smells of oil and metal chips and synthetic waxes and ozone, but mixed with them are damp earth, decay, incense, unwashed bodies, mildewed pages. There is in the air too a slight hum, electrical, and a subdued monotonous chanting. A figure in white, a man with rubber gloves, walks briskly by behind me: "Never mind. That's quite normal."

It is time now to concentrate on the lines of waiting figures. They are here for me, to receive me. I must pass down their ranks. They too are dressed entirely in white, white caps fitting tightly over their hair, gloves ready in their pockets. Though the room is generally dark, they are brilliant and clear in every feature. The weak light coming through the glass floor concentrates on them in a peculiar way, leaving the darkness around them.

Composed, discreet, I look carefully at each as I pass down the corridor they form. I know every one. They are the important people.

Each wears a large pair of spectacles, the round lenses replaced, seemingly, with mirrors reducing the size of the reflections. For in each I see an image of myself. I can make it out quite clearly, though it is very small. There too I am walking briskly down the long hall. But there is a difference: I notice that my head is placed backwards on my shoulders and I am looking toward the end of the temple where I entered. My expression is slightly puzzled and I seem to be looking for something in the distance. But neither I nor my reflection can see what it is.

IF I AM VERY careful—my head back, my arms out with the palms up, my knees flexed a little—I can just float. For a time, it cannot last long, I know, something always comes to upset the unstable balance. But, for a time...and I can look toward freedom, though it is only a rough round hole of sky, a hole so small, cutting out so much of the light of the sky, that sometimes while it is full daylight I think I can make out a star as it passes quickly by. Here is my moment of peace, when the struggling has stopped, when my surroundings and my senses rush away from me like being at the center of a silent explosion. A moment for release...Let the waters well up, float me away to the eternal motionless heaven.

But that glimpse of sky betrays me. Like a dying top, the tunnel of light reaching down to me begins to wobble and with a violent wrench is gone. Again I confront the dark stinking waters, the slippery walls, the rising waves of heat and cold. And I struggle for every breath and heartbeat through the pain.

Far above me I can see for an instant, against the madly flying rag of sky, heads peering down into the gloom. Voices distorted and hollow, echoing against the sweating walls. But I cannot listen. The pain squeezes in on me, soaks through my flesh, fills the cavities of my bones. I writhe against the bonds which shackle my feet and outstretched hands.

Where is the old I, so assured, in control?

I can still see the image of my darkened room, the medicine tray, the apple-wood posts at the foot of my bed—where they have taken me to struggle or die alone after hopeless weeks in hospitals. It is a dim image, but enough.

And my mind can still repeat ceaselessly: if I am saved, if I escape...no longer every energy on success ...enjoyment too, happiness...

I wrap myself around prayer. The formulas come. There is an intercession...

I can feel the wound in my side. It has drained me. Light, so I feel no support, but suspended rather than floating, hung by a single nerve from the sky which now opens brilliantly all about.

* * *

IT IS OVER NOW. Five score, almost. Not like Papá, but then, he...I have been useful to the end, he only a vegetable. I have been happy—she would say lucky and blessed. Happy, a full life, given and been given. The world a better place and I have played my part. God is generous and perfecting.

I am at the end. This time it is not the uncontrollable pain, or the drowning deep in the well, or the nagging of malfunctions...The long slide, planned, comfortable by schedule. The procession of family, of the important people, of the lesser seeking reflected importance. Rewarding, gratifying.

Yet I have time to remember still, to content myself with my achievements. Systematically, even, I can look back...to carry with me to the end. I shall arrange my memories lovingly...so much to be thankful for. Shapes are bending over me now, murmuring. How many times have I seen such shapes and forced myself to respond. But this time, have I not earned some indulgence? They will only think that I am again wandering or in a coma.

Family, call them to me, fondly.

FATHER, MY Papá. Watery blue eyes are looking down on me, silently, handing me the silver coin for my birthday: savings, thrift, management, my present...The gold coins for each director, "Save them, gentlemen, save them." Ideals, to be honored and passed on, never deviating. The marvelous brain, admitting nothing but the pursuit of production for the progress of mankind. Happiness meant idleness to him. Purpose, purpose. "You will learn nothing staring out the window, young man, accomplish nothing. The mind, that's what we have. Use it, train it." But it was I who drove the business on, expanding twelvefold since his day, while he redefined principles, worked in the backwaters, at cross-purposes. "I see no reason to change my views," he would say. "Human nature and the morality necessary to control it remain the same. I certainly do not agree with you. We shall not adopt your motion...I have never allowed myself to become sick and had hoped you would not either. Seek far enough and you will always find the justice of things. Liquor, tobacco, indulgence in traveling and sports and recreation (a dishonest word). Principles, the true ones..."

AND NOW I see him in his green plush arm chair by the fireplace, a small fire burning, the children in line to be received between *1995* the bony knees, the wet and smelly kiss, a speechless barrier of mutterings and tremblings and squirminess and creases too deep for the nurse's razor.

Or the undeviating determined look as he strides down the brick sidewalks, facing outward toward the spires of the University where he is soon to be granted an honorary degree, philosophy. Undeviating, unquestioning, knowing, never relinquishing. The same look that will not see the blind man selling pencils. The same knowing that will never give to the great charities, or accept the rewards and subsidies of government. He will give everything, and it is not much, to the Society: moldering, squawking its moral messages to no one, opposing everything, enjoying nothing but its own defeats...

But books have already been written about him, and there will be more...

THE CALL BELL, little silver dome with the counterbalanced button on top, on the table by each brown leather chair. The same type as a hotel porter's, but ours bear the engraved EC, Explorers Club, and our technique is not the shrill double or triple summons for the newly-employed bellhop, but a soft single tap of authority and respect for unobtrusive loyal service. We expect it, of course. "The old world, the past century, the colonial tradition, the last symbol of the gentleman—I should pay double the dues to keep those little bells."

19 39

Uncalled-for remark, nonsense, now that I think of it, even our club has its fools. These bells are efficient—portable, quiet, but incisive, bringing service. There's no sense in making more of it than that.

But tonight I do not tap it for the brandy. Papá sits in our circle of the most important members. It's the first time, I believe, that he has ever been here—though of course one does not confirm that with him. He a traveler, the Explorers Club, quite absurd! But I shall leave it to someone else to gibe him. It never succeeds. His round little eyes would open a fraction further, his nostrils suck in, his voice squeak like resin. And age, deafness, conviction, and a tempered mind, would combine to humiliate and cut down any such attempt.

In any case, I, his son, am to be the speaker.

The club seems subdued, especially so, this evening. The tobacco smoke seems thinner, the summonses for drinks even more discreet and distant, the murmurs respectful. But it is all rather hazed and meaningless. I am no longer impressed by Father, no longer brought urgently into his influence by his watery unfocused look. I'm aware of my fixed-grin pre-speech detachment, cold hands and a jumpy stomach, and my self-reassurances—I am worth any three of them except the old man, and I made him too.

For me, this exploring is only an occasional recreation, for them the intensity of the lifetime amateur.

Yet I beat them at their own game and without all the paraphernalia, even the old heroes. So it will not be difficult tonight except for Papá. With this audience I need not use the off-color jokes or pull myself to some other level. Most of them know already about my expedition, too. No need for this; I can relax…silly… must get full control…Papá I can handle afterward. He has lost his old formidability, his outrage has no importance.

"How do I find the time, you ask? The trick is to combine business and pleasure. Wolframite and scheelite, tungsten for the filaments of our light bulbs, you know. We're always looking for more of it in economic deposits. We'd got wind of an interesting possibility some fellow, an independent, had turned up on one of those aerial mineral surveys. Two or three spots, in fact. Along the river, where there were outcroppings or areas where the jungle floor was much thinner. And I'd known too that there was a lot to be done in that basin: tribes, better mapping of the river hazards, samples, and perhaps some surprises, though it had been done before, but inadequately recorded—oddly enough by a priest and poet; defrocked later, but that's another story… Yes, yes, I shall after all, why not? Brandy. Might even help me along. Ha ha!… Business-expensed a good deal of it too: Company geologist, equipment, wife was my own expense—wrong kind of business, though you might make an argument..."

I can feel my leer, refined, practiced—I loathe it and I do it. The fixed grin, the genteel guffaws—why can I not be the frightened prude I am?... Shake it off, nonsense...

"It's harder to find, these days, the travel objective to match the business. Many fingers, many pies, but you explorer types have poked around pretty thoroughly by now. Still, I've got one or two ideas."

Over the balcony at the dark end of the room I make out the form of our dusty elephant head, trunk stretched out trumpeting over his yellow tusks... They're like the novels their generation wrote, the ones who shot all these heads. And there are still a good many of them around, inherited the means and the style, still hanging on... Brandy burns down into my throat and stomach...

"...with a boy at each end poling frantically. I shall be interested to hear just what sort of rafts you used. But do tell us how in Lord's name you find time from your office and your business trips. Even if business does take you near interesting places."

I can see Papá sink deeper in his chair—the weight of disapproval—moisture freezing in his eyes. This is my opportunity, though. I'll risk his senile arguments. And there are one or two here, even here, who will pass it on to the important ones. Bit of arrogance, they'll probably call it, but the important ones, they'll know better... But how? The effective pause, fingers drumming on the leather, the hesitation. And...

"There's no trick to it, old man; you just decide you're going to and then you do. I decided, many years ago. We had been expanding fast, a rash of factories in a dozen countries, several jumps ahead of our nearest competitor, moving into new fields. Took some real sleight of hand to find the money. And I nearly killed myself, Father will tell you. I ended up in a series of hospitals, one after another could find nothing and would send me on as hopeless. Fever, terrible pains, figured I must have picked up some unknown disease on one of my trips. They finally gave me up for lost and sent me home. I was completely out of my mind, delirious, for two months. Then in a clear spell they told me they were going to operate once again, one final try—a long shot. That's when I decided. If given another chance I would no longer give everything I had to the business. It came to me crystal clear that I had been a fool, that there were other things I might like to do than knock myself out to pile up another million only a few coins of which I would ever see. I'd keep the show going, but power and size would no longer be everything. I decided I didn't have to be the best."

They're thinking it, I'm sure. Perhaps, if I put on the right sort of smile, chuckling softly at myself, not to be taken quite seriously, someone will say it. Might cut the trouble with Papá too.

Here it comes. "My God! But look, old boy, your equation hasn't quite worked out, has it? I read the financial news." I leave it with a shrug, busy with my brandy snifter. Through the fumes, my eyes smarting, I try to smile affectionately at Papá...

FFECTION, I cling to it now. It sustains me and justifies me more than I should have thought possible. Yet how much more is *1995* there left? Reach back through the veils, lifting them aside. Carefully, they are so fragile. How much have I earned? My friend, I called him my friend, yet he is dead and I did nothing. I could only listen to his last voice, as remote as another world. My father, he lies unanswered, abandoned from the beginning by the very progress he embraced, a curiosity and a nuisance. Could the rheum be tears, and would he have me ask? The last review. Memories become shadows, threatening. And I cannot turn back. Am I to be deceived by my indulgence? I am alone, the murmurings isolate me. May I turn to God to see reflections of my love? But He is not available, for I have prayed only to a convenience, a symbol in the infinite equations. My word was only an accommodation...If I but knew the features of these shadows, these mortal dangers, and the defenses. I feel the infernal opening beneath me and I am alone. Repent and they will receive you even to the last. That is what they are saying. Even without the formulae. Yet it is done, it is finished, it is final. How can it be undone? Repentance is honest only if it is preparation for the future, and I am dying. So I must accept immortality or I am lost... I cannot...another lie...

I feel my forefinger curl, my thumb poised by the knuckle, the tip of my nose becomes conscious—absurd, the old habit, aristocratic reflection, the knowing pose. Lies. Behind the gesture, hold the tip of the nose lightly, there will be time to work it out. But now I am too weak, I cannot...

The other values? The success, the envy, the power, the benefits, the well-being, the sacrifices, the tasks accepted in the spirit of public duty, the great philanthropies, the monuments which will last. Record enough? For what? To justify? Happiness, the full use of opportunities, the maximum contribution? But my questions and answers are circling. To have met the code, that would be simple, but I destroyed the old code, the standards which Papá leaned on so completely, when I made my vow, and I can no longer define a new...Yet this is all of no use. It is reason, it is mind; but it is the body that dies...

My dearest wife. Had I forgotten you? Where shall I see you? It is you that can bring peace—I should not have forgotten. But where will you be? There is time now. I shall close my eyes against the white walls, my ears against unwanted voices, my mind against justifications. I shall join you—patience, understanding, my sunlight. You refill my heart when it seems spent in doubt. I shall reach up to touch you. Take me with you, that will be enough. If I have done nothing else, I have loved you...

I

T IS A WEAKNESS, my boy, sentimentality. Do not let it get the better of you. Keep your eye always clear for the great goals. Honesty, progress, achievement, the morality man has evolved at such great cost."

That's what he might have said. I do not forgive myself that evening at the Club. His wounded, abandoned, hating look when I told of the pledge I made during my illness, it was the beginning of his final silence, hardly showing recognition.

The auditorium darkens, the monotonous rise and fall of my voice describes the route to the headwaters. Scenery, native, specimens slide back and forth on the screen. And his silent condemnation presses on me in the close air. Like two spells. One coming from some black far corner of the audience, contentious, inflexibly disapproving, reasoned and final, casting uneasiness in the shadows of the audience. The other coming from the brilliant screen and the tap of my lecturer's pointer and the rattling of my voice, casting a glow of light and attention on the crowding faces—light reflecting, reflections of projections, images trapped in the jungles by my camera; speech by the accepted formula of jargon and vulgarities and boastful understatement. Who can challenge either spell? Only he and I, from opposites, from across the crowded pit. Each, because each alone knows his world and has renounced the other's.

I CAN REMEMBER the events of that evening but do I remember my state of mind? It is only on this deathbed that I have become aware of the realities beside appearances? Distracting, trivial, wasteful appearances. We follow the text, we fail to look up. There I stood, recounting two months of my life, yet surely that was quite crowded out by the jumble of minutiae. Fingerprints on the slide, the gulp of air in my stomach, an unrestrained cough, the technique of talking, tapping for the next projection, the snow falling deeper on the homeward road. Almost anything but the reality.

Can I not remember from within rather than from outside?

I would rejoin you totally, my dearest wife...The long bruising days in buses and trucks. The buffalo carts slowly lurching up the trails through the scrub ruins of the jungle. The occasional group of gray thatched huts standing on stilts high above the black dust, the scuffling pigs, and the women bare to their black skirts, winding silk off the cocoons floating in stone pots. The sick sweet smell of cassava roots being ground and the astringent smell from the cartloads of garlic and chilies. The jungle thickening, cooling, in the areas of the temples, stone blocks and ruined statues tangled in the roots and vines. There is a motion and an odor and a presence which the camera never catches...I would join you...

T HE FIRST DAY on the river. A settled area still, above the gorges and the wilder parts. *19* | *35* The river is swift and shallow over the shingle, cold from the high snow mountains, almost clear. The banks are high, eroded. Often we pass great screeching irrigation water wheels, scooping water up as they turn with the current, dumping into troughs on the tops of the banks leading off to unseen farms. We float with the current in our long line of bamboo rafts, each with its leaf-roof shelter in the center and an irregular deck at each end where the raft men pole or squat. One raft is the cookhouse with its dugout canoe to paddle breakfast to us. For lunch we line up on a sandbar where the farmland dwindles into the jungle. In the distance the hills begin. Before sunset we pull into the bank above the last remote village. While the rafts are being staked to the bank and supper prepared, we walk down to the village. No longer farming people, this is a hill tribe which moves down seasonally for the best fishing. Goatskins about their loins, red clay marking on their foreheads, one old man with a rudimentary bagpipe. We persuade him to play for a tape recording. The group that collects we photograph with flashes. Campfires are burning in the sand when we return, the men squatting around them in order of seniority. Drinking-water basins are scooped a step back from the river's edge, the water flowing up into them clear, filtered by the sand. Rice liquor, chicken roasted on green spits, bamboo shoots, tea, pineapples. The fires die, the men wander off to sleep where they will, on the rafts, in the warm sand, with the villagers.

By the light of the paraffin lamp hanging from the ridge pole at one end of our raft shelter I write up the notes of the day, make verifications in the few books on the area which I have brought with me, store the samples we have collected. The lamp out, a half-moon lighting the river as it slides by, gurgling in the bamboo logs. We unwind the cotton patterned cloths we use for our only clothing, step silently into the water. We lie in the shallow current for a few moments, anchored to the shifting sandy bottom by fingertips. Shrunken by the cold, we sidle back to the raft. I hand you up carefully onto the slippery logs. We lie together. Through the open end of our shelter I learn the new constellations. I feel the warmth of your body....

Have I not joined you?... Judge me, forgive me.

Margaret

YOU LIE SO STILL, my husband, your eyes so far away. Your hand stirs. Would you touch *19 | 95* me? Do you listen to my tears? You were young and handsome and brave and you conquered so much. I see a shadow of fear in your eyes. Do not be afraid. Do not resist death, if that is what it be, for it is no defeat. Accept, finally; it is the only way. I call it grace, but do not mind, it need not have a name. Accept as you never have before. Only thus can man in the end return to woman and the earth.

Never before were you accepting and understanding, always the strong stroke out against the current, the denial, the peak rather than the pass, the whole rather than its detail…Accept, flow with the current. It knows best by not knowing at all, by only flowing.

You will be measuring your achievements now, yet wondering whether they count. Remembering failed affection, regretting the compromises. Your vow in your illness, a vow unkept, driving you on to seek both lives at once, both falling short—impossible goals. All man's goals are impossible, as woman knows from the beginning, and if he does not come to realize this, to accept, to rejoin with woman, he will be tormented eternally. Forget the scale, the competition, the gains and losses. Forget the privileges and powers, the theorems and abstractions, the judgments. Be grateful for your elations and fires and forces, but the only final result is the return to the uncaring earth.

Silent still, your eyes are studying the distance. I lie beside you, your body is cold and unyielding. Opposing, calculating. Moments of passion and tenderness, but too soon receding back into the mind. Why could I never have given you joy? The joy of childhood which you never knew, high spirits, reckless, irrepressibly wild. Is it too late? Your vow which I heard ringing through the house so many times, which you told me of so sweetly much later, thinking I did not know—was it the choked cry of joy seeking escape? Too late even then, for though you tried so hard you could never keep that vow or set free that cry. Sentiment is not the same, nor the moments of love or appreciation or beauty noted or generosity. Joy is generosity to one's self, unlimited and unconscious.

D
1935

O YOU REMEMBER our jungle trip on the raft? Sometimes you would lie beside me and I could feel your heart... The night bird shrilling in the jungle across the river,

153

mocking the whistle of a boy at a pretty girl, filling the
air for long moments with its echoes. A nearby thicket-
full of parrots, restless, disturbed by some prowler;
they chatter irritatedly. A breeze stirs the bamboo
thatch, soothes the jungle back to sleep. The raft shifts
slightly against the sand, riding higher, perhaps on
the bright mountain sun of many days ago—snow
washing out to the sea. Thus are we accepted in their
land.

A ferocious black pig has been bought at the last
village and for days it rides with us on the stern deck
of the cookhouse raft. You tell me, with the male pre-
sumption that I am interested and should know—no,
no! I only rarely feel that, forgive me—that pigs let
wild, in three generations, or four, or something, turn
into boars, that as cousin of the river god it is being
held as hostage against disaster, that swine in almost all
mythologies...that this, that that. But he has an evil
eye and a scream of malice and he talks to me. He tells
me, as our rafts drift near to each other in a wider calmer
stretch, that his human ancestor was a river bandit who
robbed the tan-bark boats and raped every ripe woman
he could reach. That he is immortal now. However often he is castrated and slaughtered, as was the bandit
when caught in a woman-baited trap, he returns to
wreck the riverboats and rip open the secret flesh and
feast on his own remains.

Monkeys as big as children race across the face of a crumbly pink cliff, impossibly far above, sheer to the river gnawing at its base, a few bushes and vines cropping out in the wrinkles like hairy moles on an old woman's face. Careless children on the giant decaying face of the earth, screaming at our line of rafts. Is it the way of jungle life to scream? Nothing mourns or yields or turns in on itself?

Deep in an enormous crevice of the earth, the sun has long gone. In the narrow strips of jungle along the riverbanks, cluttered with flood debris even high in the branches, the night sounds begin. The ridiculous rude man-whistle, sliding up, sliding down. The single plucked sustained note of the tiny scops owl. Far off a fearful death cry, a rabbit perhaps—I'd rather not ask than be held either ignorant or wanting to catch him ignorant—hopeless, rising up out of the river bottom, echoing and dying against the indifferent cliffs and bluffs. Above, where the sky sweeps everything into nothing, where the blue turns black quite unawares, a brilliant flame swoops and tumbles, falling, a fiery Icarus hurled down from the heavens. And suddenly the fire is quenched in shadow, a white bird sails out of the evening sun into our twilight.

Yet the flame reappears. As the hand of creation reaches forth, seeming not to touch yet imparting life—the infinite interval between lovers—so that bit torn from the sun has set fire to the earth. Rushing to reach back to the sunlight, flames sweep up the festooned vines, thunder in the branches, burst forth from the treetops, triumphant pennants, jubilant, joyful at the miracle that released them from the jungle. Heat like the sudden flush of fever, wind sucked past, whirling dust and leaves into the exultant column of fire. Wildly exhilarated faces, laughing, frenzied with shouting, gold burning on the naked black—your face, grim, shocked, planning—and I too, hesitant only for an instant of guilt, am whirled up with the flames, soundless shriek of delight. From the black behind the blazing tree—I am looking for it, listening—the death scream, silencing even the tumult of the fire, evil ripped from the brutal jungle, defiant, mocking, abusive. And the final shriek of malice, sustained until my soul is filled with its splinters, ending with a white flash and a violent explosion.

The fire burns on, darker, redder flames, glowering in the gathering night.

Brands are carried to a pit dug near the rafts. Driftwood is thrown in, flares up, lighting bared tusks, sneering lips, his black-bristled grotesque carcass dragging blood through the clean sand. Carried behind, proudly at arm's length, comes a lumpy object wrapped in a white cloth leaking blood. It is a dedication made before me—palms together and the graceful little bow behind the dangling bundle—to me, there is no one else near, you are off with your flashing camera, the river men are all busy with the sacrificial feast. From a large stone jug a glass is handed me, rice liquor, fire poured straight into the heart.

Faces are loosening, louder with their exuberance, gestures exaggerated. The judgment of the sky is hidden by bright flames, the heavy greasy smoke. The men get on with their drainings, careful divisions, choppings and grindings and poundings, pots and spits and hissing pans, slices and joints and gray pastes and black puddings. On a pointed pole back from the fire pit, tongueless, eyeless, brainless, is the slowly dripping head. Clenched in its teeth is the hairy castrated sheath. He seems cunning, looking out over the shiny bare figures to the river, their soft grunts of satisfaction. Gurgling, chuckling, spitting.

The river somewhere behind stirs, restless, worrying at the rafts, ropes groaning on their stakes, waves with the damp night wind sputtering between the logs, spittle bubbles glittering. Slight lifting, straining toward the fire; hesitant, twisting, sliding back. Slow dance, stirring secretly under the rough weaves and patterns of the night; touching and untouching, altering, drawing into points of expectancy, preparing; gentle rhythms unfolding.

The stone jug appears and reappears. You pass by,

busy with wires and rigs, flashes, reels, commands. Intent. Can this survive the blue lenses and the blindings and the winding tape? Move over, go away. Why must you stand just there? Why must you be forever doing, and so insufferably well? It is me, me, me! Don't you know I'm here? The rhythm of the river, the pulse of the earth, a hand rests lightly, or is it only a thought? But you've gone.

Voices, intonings, the earth teeters, unsteady, swaying; the pole stands fixed, still, its head glowing darkly in the light from the pit. A pause, silence, a figure comes toward me from the fire, a supple shadow quite close, a man, naked but for a white loin cloth, carrying a round wooden tray. He kneels by the edge of the raft, graceful in the sand and shallow water. I woman! But how can I be quite solemn? I am shivering with delight. Yellow flowers of the night jasmine decorate the tray. As it is lowered, steady on one hand, the other fingers extended up in the gesture of greeting, savory steams come to me. It is lowered to my lap. The only motion then is the gentle rising of the river. Suspension, the drawn breath, delight…he has vanished. Slowly, prolonging the delicious flavors, I eat the two testicles in their sweet sauces.

✻   ✻   ✻

YOUR EYES are on me now. You touch me with your eyes. I see no suffering in them, *19* | *95* but perhaps a hesitation, an uncertainty. Accept, my dear, it is the only way. And acceptance is joy.

You have tried, ever since we met and were married, I think. Other outlooks, other modes, for some departure from your parents, your righteous Papá. You have said that you saw in me...what?...yet somehow it has always eluded you.

Let it be enough that you tried. All that matters is the final acceptance.

"Give all that up!" you would say. "Art is only entertainment and diversion. Importance is power and success honestly...knowing, understanding...advancing, progressing...comforts, enlightenment...rewards, happiness."

Accept—with every measure of my will and my love I beg you. Now, though never before. Now, though not in childhood, where it should always be.

How can I help you, how can I show you the meaning of joy? Look inward and then do not look at all. Do you not feel a space spreading out around you in all directions, you helpless in this space, lacking all control, so completely that it is no longer a concern, that the very concept of control disappears? I know, I think, I ought, I was, I shall—they all drop away. I am, I accept—the state of being. That is the condition of joy. And it can be the condition of childhood and life— and death.

A cart of medicines is pushed past your door. It rattles mortally, its axle shrieks.

I 9 2 8 AM SWEPT from sleep, the cry still echoing. I want it to be the loon, his cry of love, ringing out over the gold-black lake, soul of the Northman sailing out to the moon. But the echoes are bitter with fear, and the taste is not the sweet pine pollen but the acid burning of leaf mold. Fear and death... bird to beast to man...Yet I am returned to my beloved Island, to show my children and my husband this childhood. To show it to myself, to bring it to me.

The mosquito net billows with the night wind, with the breath of the death scream. But I can forget, for a while. We have come through the hollow of time, down the lanes arched with maples, the long journey to the same home, the same porch on the lake's edge, the same bed... I watch over this me. Never fear, sleep softly, my loves, lingeringly, lovingly, at the end of the journey to our miraculous world—make sure of it, very, very sure.

Yes, this miraculous world: its secret fern-filled hollows, friendly squirrels, expeditions; the unreachable packet boat regulating our days, washing our shores twice daily with its wake from miles away; bonfires and ghost stories on the ledges; mosquito nets dropped around our beds to protect us, my sisters and me, from the owls and the lonely loon; and spiders, everywhere, every size, so many that they became accepted and even named—though my little brother did think it exciting to put several of the biggest in the bait trap to see how many days it would take to drown them. Each year we find new spider skeletons on the ceilings and walls and stretched across the filigree holes in the gingerbread. For days I think them alive. Like the time we were hiking up our picnic hill and approached a statue of a hunter standing on the highest rock. "Mother, I thought for a second that that was a real man standing there." The statue heard, smiled, walked silently away.

Midsummer, they have a party at the Farm on the mainland. We're invited by the Colonel to help, or mostly just to be there. He's a kind and generous guardian for all his gruffness.

"Keep the cows out, let the guests in." My brother is only nine, two years younger than I, but they trust him more. My sister and the other children are to show the guests to their rooms. Me, stationed out of harm, they hope, halfway down the long front porch of the Farm, fresh-painted white with orange gingerbread and trim everywhere and gleaming gray resounding floor with its weaving hemp carpet. All ribbons and pigtails and my long rustling frock—whinnying and pawing to be out cantering the stubbly hayfield, little brother at the reins. And it's not quite fair; I like so to swing on those great gates, slide their wooden bolts to, scratch designs with my thumbnail in their soft silvery rails. Counting in from the road, or for that matter from the tobacco-brown station with its peanuts machine in its stale smoky click-clacking waiting room—and I always forget my purse anyway—and we count them each trip, calling off the names we gave each for an adventure there—Evil Spirits for an owl's call and a lost doll's shoe, Sister's Shame for I guess I left it unbolted once and the farmer there said he never did find one cow and the Colonel had to pay for it, we were too poor—counting in, there are eleven in all, ten for the drivers to cope with and then the last gate at the end of the back pasture where the stallion is and where I would be if...

But now the guests begin to arrive and I am glad I am here after all. Oh! the horses, usually in pairs, tossing about because they know they have arrived and they smell the oats in the barn across the drive. The farmer's oldest boy holds their heads while the guests get out, then leads them to the end of the lengthening line of unhitched carriages, unharnesses them and lets them out in the paddock to water and roll and sneeze in the dust. I call to them silently, greet them, leaning out over the porch rail, and they know that I am paddocked too and sometimes snort back and stare fiercely at me.

And the ladies, all kinds of hats, parasols, billowy formless dresses so beautiful. The men handsome in their caps and golfing knickers, excited like little boys. One or two great shaking coughing automobiles too, brass and paint and passengers all blurred with the white dust. But they are nothing compared to horses.

The Colonel—everyone calls him that, even his own wife, funny chippering never-finished Aunty—greets them out under the elm, flanked by the foreman-farmer. In the lulls the two of them chat, sitting in their canvas campaign chairs in the shade. Aunty, Mother, and the other ladies of the Farm are to appear later when everyone has rested, changed, and assembled for afternoon punch.

For these greetings they stay far apart, as if they were reaching over a hedge, to avoid the embarrassment of the streaks of sweat and the dust and the smudges. Then, referring to a chart he pulls from his pocket, he sends them off, escorted by one of the children: day guests to rooms in the Farm, weekend guests distributed among the guest houses on the edge of the lake down through the fields of corn and hay. The farmer explains the arrangements and the guest-house shuttle-carriage system to the servants—each weekend group brings one or two—supervises his boy with the horses, and takes the drivers around to the back porch.

For the moment there are no carriages in sight, the Colonel has gone into the Farm. I swing over the porch rail, race out into the hot four o'clock sun, bounce once in the coachman's seat of the most elegant carriage, climb to the top rail to kiss the velvet nose of a great gray who has thundered over to see me. A wet blasting whinny betrays me.

The boy calls in a loud kind of whisper, "Hey! Scat or he'll catch you!"

I slide off the fence, but a ribbon on my front catches and tears, dangling, The boy sees, skitters over, snips it off completely with his pocket-knife and you'd hardly notice. But too late. A rattling roaring laughing cloud was bouncing up and the Colonel appears in the doorway.

"Young lady!" That's enough. He likes everything just so and I'm not, hardly ever I guess. So she'll be chosen instead of me to set the duckpins in the bowling alley later in the afternoon.

The refreshments—punch, strawberries with great globs of fresh cream, cook's special cookies—are spread out on deal tables on the side porch and on the croquet lawn under the elms and maples. Aunty appears, and Mother, and there is a lot of chattering and posturing and pretty ladies and mustaches and even a four-piece orchestra. After a while there is a kind of bugle call played on the piano, the call they use to signal a horse race. The drum rolls, the farmer's boy sets off a pinwheel firecracker on a pole sticking up out of the birdbath, and the Colonel steps out to the porch rail to announce the program for the rest of the day.

We all start for the lake, children and some of the younger grownups on foot, the others shuttled by the Farm's carriages. First the bowling. Bowling House, by Boathouse Beach, has just been finished and it is all gleaming and sporting its magnificent orange gingerbread.

The Colonel relented: my sister and I are perched up between the two pits, duckpins flying, squeals, though Mother had sleeve-tugged the Colonel to send the farmer's boy instead—really rather dangerous. It's awfully hot and soon there's rummaging in wicker baskets, bathing costumes produced. Changing in Bathhouse then much splashing and breast-stroking, the older people only walking out thigh-deep, scooping water onto their arms and faces, dipping to their necks for a moment.

Out from Boathouse comes Steamer. Even it has no name. You just have to kind of capitalize your voice. The Lake means the whole thing: Farm, Guest House

One, and so forth, Island, Point, Boathouse, everything. Without the capitals, the "lake" is just the lake, and the "farm" is where farming is done.

Two or three big rowboats are pushed out through the piles under the side of the Boathouse and are sculled over to the Landing. There is a clamor in deciding who goes in what. We know we shall not be allowed to row or even steer, so as passengers we decide to go on Steamer. The rowboats go on ahead while we are still loading up.

She is lovely, all white and orange, of course, with a gleaming big brass smokestack, square cabins and round windows and all over decked out with pennants and the orchestra already tuning up on the roof. One of the Colonel's sons—we just call them "Sir," but the grownups almost always speak of them together as just the "Colonel's Sons" and say they "don't amount to much" and they seem to me to be just big silly children who play too rough, though they're as old as Mother—one of them is Captain and there are lots of blasts of the whistle and screams about forgotten parasols—because they think they're becoming, I guess, there isn't much sun left—and a great flowery hat falls into the lake and we are off.

While the rowboats can go along inside the Island through the Narrows, we have to go out around, and even then they say it is very tricky with a big boat. Every rock and ledge and shallows has a marker on it:

an iron pole drilled into it somehow, even when they are way underwater, and on top a bright orange thing, each different—a ball, or a cube, or a cross, or a triangle. Along one channel there's a heart, a club, a diamond, and a spade, and at another place, over by Sally's Gut, well outside the Colonel's usual limits—I guess that's why it has such a nice name—an Eiffel tower, a silhouette of a lady without any clothes on, a poodle dog, and a champagne bottle. So the channels and hazards are known by the names of their markers, and the Colonel's Sons have almost a language of their own as they navigate about. How wonderful, daring, victorious we are, steaming about through these waters! There are tiny pined islands here and there, miles and miles of bays and headlands and beaches and narrow marsh-like passages, wild with the spirit of the North People, now and then a farm clearing down to the lakeside, one or two camps. And Steamer pushing out her wake everywhere, whistle echoing in the forests, music-hall tunes, brassy in the sunset.

We're kind of boasting, maybe, but everything is so sure and successful and there's so much room. "The new era, proud and right," that's what the Colonel says.

We aren't going far. A short detour past Girl's Camp. Jokes and laughter. Then round the Deep Hole end of the Island and across the bay to the Landing out near the end of the Spindle Point. The rowboats have already arrived. The Landing, the Colonel has built that too, just this year. A barge brought in the granite, and he did Lighthouse at the same time. We haven't seen it yet and we're so excited we nearly miss the sweet roast corn, rushing off to inspect it, climb its spiral stairs, cry out at landmarks from its lightless top.

You serve yourself. There is even a tablecloth on the long planks-on-sawhorses table, with china plates, the corn, heaps of butter, baked salmon so good that even we like it, an enormous salad in Aunty's punch bowl, and bowls of sliced peaches and the cream again. It has all been brought out in the biggest farm wagon. They'd fixed up the old lumber road over Lookout Hill and down through the woods all the way to the end. The grownups sit around on folding chairs and log benches, and we race and gobble and whoop out of earshot and skip stones on the other side of the Point, the stormy side. When the sky has faded quite away and we can just see the last skimming dying of our best throws, there is a very loud and jumpy explosion behind us. We all remember and cry "Fireworks!"

Steamer has pulled out a bit into the lake, they have put some kind of platform on her roof, and they are setting off the fireworks there. We can see it as we dash back through the black pine trunks, and a white pinwheel flashing in the ripples urges us to hurry.

Flashes and stars and sprays like your eyes tight shut.

The awful bangs as if your lungs had burst, as if your knees had been kicked out from behind. I'm curled on the prickly pine needles, and I can't bear to look and I can't bear not to look, and I press my palms to my ears to keep out doomsday. Finally there is silence and darkness. As I cautiously lift my hands free a tiny fraction, there is a great swoosh of fire and three bright streaks loop out over the stars and bang and bang-bang almost on top of each other, and they spiral and burst and shower, and three parachutes float free, lit by flares, rose and green and bright blue, dangling three ships in full sail. They land far out in the lake, lights spluttering still, and we are allowed by the Colonel to row out and rescue them and squabble over them and bring them to show the grownups.

By the time we've rowed rather meanderingly back, Steamer has tied up again at the end of the pier. The orchestra tunes up again, lanterns are hung from poles and from the stubby fake mast and yardarms. The Colonel and Aunty lead off in a bouncy polka. Somehow, the evening is no longer ours.

We walk silently, our feet can't help but step with the music, to Lighthouse. From up here it seems almost as if the pier, planked over for the dancing, were a great royal barge floating on the river of rivers, we in our stony castle wishing with all our might to grow up so that we too could whirl and whirl in our floating dresses in the arms of a baron or a gypsy or a prince to the violins and the soft splashing of the waves—my sister and I, at least, little brothers would be more interested in the accordion and in trying to make us believe there really is a bat here.

Too soon they find us and pack us into the wagon with the leftovers—Mother too, so she can take us out to the Island. For a time I feel quite poisonous, thinking up revenges and making promises to myself about when I'm grown up. From the top of Lookout Hill we can see the lights again. The wind brings us a few farewell notes.

An owl calls, the forest closes in tight…We are early settlers moving on into the north country, making use of the moonlight too to find our new homes before the long winter catches us…

We're out of the wagon and into our rowboat. Mother is rowing, slowly, the others seem asleep. The steering paddle makes a sluicing sound, sending up a skin of water on my fingers—warm in the night air. It's cramped and hard but I dare not move because the rest of the seat is cold and slimy with dew.

Quite suddenly I am in bed—lost, somehow, a whole piece of my life. Through the railing cut like the slots in violins, I think I can see, like fireflies on a twig, lights dancing on the tip of the long black finger of the Point.

It is darker. Something woke me. Was it the setting

of the moon? Something cold and lonely like the last
note of the loon as he leaves forever. I pull the covers up
higher to be safe, curled with my wrists tight between my
knees. The mystic protection—it has always saved me.

Wild strawberries—they grow in patches, shady where
the grass is short, in unused fields and along the thin
edges of the woods. We have spread out, each in a different direction, to pick some for the guests. I have found
delicious ones in the shade of a cherry tree in an old
pasture behind the Ice House. Perhaps the rotting sawdust which they throw out whenever they dig down
for a new block of ice, and which has spread all about,
makes a particularly good bed for them. They grow
thickly and are riper, warm in the afternoon sun. Just
beyond the trunk of the tree are the rails of the fence,
grown over with blackberries and honeysuckle, sepa-
rating the pasture from the pine forest beyond. There's
a kind of ditch behind the fence, hidden. It must have
been a brook bed. Perhaps the sawmill up the valley
took its water away into another course, I don't know.

When you first see a strawberry patch you reach
down to pick a few. But if it's a good one it will pull
you right down to your hands and knees and even flat
to your stomach and elbows. That's how I am now.
Hunting in the tangles of grasses and weeds for the
hiding berries. How can I not just eat them straight

off? A little later, then I'll start putting every other one in the basket, just a little later.

Voices, almost beside me it seems, they must be down in the ditch. A woman, "Oh why did I choose to come back in that rowboat! It must have been so exciting. Tell me about it from the beginning, you must or I'll leave this minute."

I know who will answer, with his bullying voice. "Well, it wasn't long after we'd left—we had had to go back for those two. They said they were up in Lighthouse and no one told them we were going. And I'd pulled that whistle myself I bet a dozen times. You'd know what they were up to! Screamed like a couple of stuck pigs when they saw us pulling out.

"I was at the wheel, going along at a good clip, heading for Jew's Star, when I saw it swimming quite a way ahead of us, clear in the moonlight. Soon we could tell it was a doe, heading for the Island from somewhere over near Birch Point. I yelled and wheeled around after her, everybody laughing by then and shouting and someone had the orchestra play bugle calls. I missed the first time, dodged me, everybody jeered, but it wasn't easy a bit. We heeled way over circling around too sharp after her—I was mad—and I thought I had lost her for a bit. But we made it. I spotted the splashing about. That was when I yelled into the megaphone. Guess she knew the game was up. Just kind of stopped there and

I got her square—amidships, you might say. She let out that shriek you heard, just before we hit her, like a thousand factory whistles. Still floating, so we towed her home. Eat her tomorrow, though she'll be green."

I CURL INTO MY warmth, deeper in the blankets, peeking. The netting shivers, crystal fragments of a cry glitter in the purple sky. The loon and the deer, their voices have joined. Their cry guards my miraculous world, fixing it forever. A moment held in the unknowable pattern of the stars...So I have failed you, my husband, my son. I cannot regain a moment; it has passed into my immortality and is not yours. I supposed...how was it? That the Lake would evoke my world for you to borrow?

But what do you see? An old time, lost and dead, at best a little world, unaware of its destiny, unwilling to look beyond? Decaying now, to be replaced? Already the first signs, life renewed on a different basis, clearing away, rationalizing, developing, progressing? Can I ever show you that only the moment is attainable, that the only goal is the ungoal? Or should I try? Will your vow—talked of so boastfully now—leave you in a void, unable to fully grasp any world? I am afraid for you, my dearest husband, and I have failed you, failed either to carry you on through some great rush of accumulating achievements which I could never understand, or to hold you in the embrace of the moment.

And my son, what is this to you? Uncomfortable, distasteful, forced uncomprehendingly? Deer flies driving you to a frenzy at Evil Spirits. Sour cream smell—and you aren't allowed to have any—in the old billiard room where the separator howls on its electric motor. Wet sneakers and mosquitoes in the unkempt fields stretching down to the lake—it would be simple to build a road and a bridge out to the Island. Guest Houses shuttered blind and meaningless, Bowling House ajar, rotted open, a few duckpins to roll crazily, in the stink of the swallows' nests. Boathouse dark with green light coming in through the water, throwing terrifying masks on our faces until the great door is heaved open…and you are blinded and angry because you're told you know what you don't know. Heaving supplies into the boats, last one's feet wet. And the Island, sullen, inhospitable, fringed with a black tangle of evergreens and ledges and alders devoured by caterpillars. The Deep Hole at the far end where the rocks cut sharp into the lake. Where every morning, Johnny my son, before breakfast you have to swim with your father, naked. Exposing your tight white nothingness, all the careful unconcern, eyes elsewhere. Exposure, display—I have more of her than you. Brown water bottomless before the sun, then dimly the deep tangle of snags in the leafy slime. And the stains of blood, fish scales, where you bang and bang their heads, held prickly by the tail, feel the life writhe out; struggle sick with a pocket knife through the belly, cold gray guts; cleaning, your father calls it, and it is all washed away, eaten by other fish. Shivering on the edge for the awful dive, knees half-bent, wishing to curl into some dark secret, hands clasped pressed to thighs, elbows touching, wrists hiding you, giggling: no! you go first, with your great things flinging about. And you too—into that shocking pit where the dead trails slowly in blurred spirals forever halfway from the green waving sun to the bony bottom.

How can I rescue you, Johnny my son?

Johnny

HALFWAY. Suspended in the gloom. Water *19 33* to cold brown air, dimly the rough rock wall curving from the light down to the final floor. Withholding a return to either. Reserving even identification. I the common interval, I plural, I general, I neutral. "How can I rescue you" echoing. Half immersed and free, half bound still to the surface. Like the edge of a dream which can still be recaptured and even controlled.

I THE SON, I have stood by the bedside too, lis*1 9 9 5* tened to the currents, but he has not joined them. What do I see as I look down on them? Is head supplanting hand? Are these lifetimes only delusion, are any lives not? Are not doubts always met with justifications, formulas? And if they are not, is the deliberately unmet doubt in itself a formula? Can any one truly accept?

She, my mother, she sits by him, heavy with sleep and sadness, rounded, softened into indistinct shapes enfolding the original clear pattern, yet with a final force turning back instinctively to her original, trying to bring him to it again, disregarding the years of concession, of bewildered half-agreement, of gradual attrition, years of he-must-be-right accumulating, years of joining, of going to him. "She's a saint martyred to his ambitions and drives and principles," finally loses all meaning. Love could do it.

She is revealed, though, revealed by one surviving trait: she could never accept, or give, the fruits of success. "Why should this be ours? Do we deserve this? How can I be generous with what really is not mine because it should not be? How lucky we are!"

Her delusion of virginity.

He, my father, jaw slacked open, his palate clicks with each shallow breath. His eyes are closed, but a slit of white escapes. Yellow, unshaven now that the procession has ended, fetid. Do only the violent or the saintly or the alone avoid the ugliness of death? Merciful, comfortable, over quickly—like a tooth extraction. Or would he prefer the consuming demands of the unendurable pain?

For all the triumphs, the achievement of carefully renounced goals, the power, the farewells, the evidence of respect and love—this is the end. He was not used to doubts, fears, yet he is honest and will have them now. He has lived too long, for his set of answers is endangered. Perhaps he can avoid this, though, even without the pain, drawing himself in behind his old vow, persuading himself that it had meaning and that he kept it.

Executive limousines purr at the curb, gray uniforms, dispatch cases, close-tolerance clicks. Glass doors swing open in reflex to the cut beam of the photoelectric eye. Hats are proper, brushed, except for yours, Father—the illusion of the vow—shielding the infrared heat in the entrance ceiling. Doors again, generous nicknaming and gratifying overpayment for the out-of-town newspaper. More goodwill to the elevator boy, who answers Mister. Smiles to permit full value from elbow-rubbing the Chief. Subdued preparations along the corridor to the hum and the faint chlorine odor of the water cooler. Doors casually open to allow extra recognition. Outer office girls poised and elegant and friendly, earning more than a vice-president thirty years ago, you would say.

I957 S THAT ART? But they said it had to be—prestige, right spirit, everything comes in under the corporate roof these days; otherwise...the corner view. The Park, hard going now, switching to Arts Center, more money. The University, the old twisting and bulbing towers dwindling under the glassy skins. The river black and empty under the looping interchanges, the bond-issue bridge already overcrowded... Architecture carefully shields the sun.

The walls are photographically wallpapered, one side with odd-angle views of the production line of the latest factories, the other a bamboo raft going through heavy rapids. The picture of the honorary degrees together with the Prime Minister remains... "Tell him to chair it, I may be down...Responsibilities of public ownership, duties to the stockholders, community-minded, an enlightened force in the political and international scene, no longer only production and growth, agreements within the law, the important people....

"I'm amazed that you would even think it within your responsibilities, but then to...boy to do a man's job...common sense...not the way I learned it... doesn't anyone else around here? The right to get angry at subordinates. The right to have subordinates...

"Have a seat, five minutes yet—put our feet up... Utility, that's the measure in production, and that's the measure in human affairs. If ever I were to cease to be useful that's the time to die, not later... What's the secret? Why, it's knowing what's important and what's unimportant... Of course, in fact I took the picture. But that's important—relaxation, and particularly perspective.

"Yes, I know the objections. We're fouling our nest. Destroying, unplanned, uncontrolled. Loss of the human value, the individual. The cult of the mass, and so forth. The genocides and ceaseless wars of rivalry. Headstretchers proliferating, the nut-houses filling up, moral standards disappearing. Always been pessimists around, sometimes I skirt close myself. But, but, but. Look around. It's a big place still, we just have to keep moving, as we always have, for that matter. And at the same time you simply can't write off the improved welfare, the comforts, the security, the exploding knowledge, that our energies have brought. We'll find new ways and new frontiers. And we've got to get used to having the masses much more obvious than before. We can always find new exclusivenesses when we need them."

YOUR DELUSIONS of virginity, Father.

19 | 95 I shan't argue. You have always granted interviews to me, Father, rather than discussions—and to her too. Only the deathbed debate is left you. No, that's not in malice, rather almost envy, though your absolution could be made easier if you could entertain religion again. I see you're busy, I am going. But look, I must tell you something.

In that Board room, where she had me wait—was it not a brand new building, just moved in? Elegant, simple, almost bare, I was impressed. But, as I waited, doodling on the chairman's pad, thinking about nothing at all—something I should never admit to you—I heard a strange grinding noise, very faint, under the table. It kept on. I leaned over rather suddenly, somehow a little scared and wanting to dispel it. There, just at my feet, was a large black rat, lips drawn back, gnashing his teeth.

Lowell

P ROLONGING, adjusting—as a fish would his *19 95* air bladder to hold him motionless at some critical and most essential level, not daring to subside to the slimy bottom or rise up through the murk to the cruel and killing surface in the sun. But it is cold and the effort tiring. I'll take a moment of rest to regain strength, float free from this impossible balance, whether falling or rising—through the slow currents, drifting past blurred translucent shapes, suggestions settling. The light increasing, intenser— drawn to it, it draws together. From a general stratum of less gloom it gathers into a single source, ringed, pulsing, heavy with its gravity...Is it too late?

Hovering forms, moths about a light, behind is the straining, the staring, dimmer, the iris reflex. Would they drive their light full into my skull, quenching it in my brain? Let me stare out into that world for a time yet. I dare not close my eyes, too weary to squint. Let me be a while yet. Your light is a vice crushing my eyeballs. Release, in the name of God! Release! Leave me! With my dying soul I implore you! Leave me be, with your tamperings and tests and hoverings. How

could you not know death when it is the end of everything? Or is it the beginning? But it is too late to doubt.
I must prepare, concentrate, prepare, find the essential
to carry with me. Where is it, where?. . . The beginning
is the end. Turn back. Turn inward. . . Wisdom is doubt,
doubt kills death. Back to conviction, force, enthusi-
asm, where the source of the source is unknowable,
where the line runs straight, where the future is attainable. . . I was right once. . . .

My flesh shudders and clings about my bones, and
my bones are shaken violently. . .ridding, releasing.

Touch of Dust

Manlio

HE SKY is darkened by the rifts in heavy
clouds off to the south. Rain slants in
sweeps of gray across wild waves. The
breakwater is black under the exploding
attacks of the Adriatic, churning white foam. Out near
the end is a strange structure like an enormous cage of
nightmares, a fishing crane, splintered, dangling in the
surf. To windward a great ship struggles close-hauled
clawing to fetch clear of the rocks, seems to be losing,
driven back toward the savage breakers, jeered at by
the shrieks of a bird filling half the leeward sky, beak
twisted open, black tongue spitting out, and a single
eye, flaming red.

That is the only brilliant color, a touch with my
finest brush, in the somber storm...that eye watching
as the storm crashes through into my bedroom and
rages about me, breaks over me, hurls me and my easel
against the walls, watching as it storms into my brain
and fills me with joy...Color, you scraggly old bird,
you didn't see me as you flapped into the storm, but I
saw you and caught the anger of your eye. Now red
and flame orange and white flare up the shrouds and

halyards and braces, burst into the reefed and close-hauled canvas, out along the yards. I hear the sputtering of the caked salt, I smell the burning tar, I see the stilled faces and the terrified faces.

But to defy you, and because there is a corner of my heart still calm in the storm, I put in a splendid yellow that lights the low clouds, and somehow I can tell that the ship will never wreck, never be completely devoured by your fire. And you, malignant bird, will hang there forever, unanswered.

Or the rain can be soft and carry a light of its own and fall untroubled, like love. From a frosted silver sky, through the shining golden leaves of the poplars, down the black trunks, collecting bright on a green umbrella. Steam soaking in the oily smelly wool, bunched together for warmth and protection. White puddles, and the smell of autumn dust rising up through the rain...I paint smell; it is in the way the light reflects on the air, in the temperature of the air, in its drift and weight...

Yes, there is the weight of a particular light. I measure it, note it on my sketch pad. And secretly I apply it with my paints onto the canvas. Depending on its direction, it pushes objects forward or back in the scene, pressing down or releasing. It is pressure on things. And some terribly strong lights have no pressure at all, while others can crush, or throw things in your face. The faintest light can sometimes be as heavy as conscience on execution dawn... My father defended him well, worked hard, though believing him guilty, and he lost to the hood and the noose and the floor dropping into the sky. My father joined in a legal murder. I would have thrown my life to the accused's defense...an unmarked stone in an unknown field.

I fly away on my bicycle, escaping from the smell of death in the parlor, off to my friend the fisherman where he is hiding and waiting for me and for the wine and buns and chicken breasts I bring him. Spinning through the market place, past carts and carriages and women lost under their great fluffy hats, and dogs and skipping children and chickens and lines of mules going out for firewood, and a rich man's throbbing automobile; past churches and pot shops and millions of caged songbirds, and a knife grinder on his bicycle, and lines of orphans going out for air, and a beggar's hat turned up on his trembling knees. Out through half-blind gates, and on.

From stone and shadows into the light, from cobbles and gutters into the dust and weeds and late spring flowers and the frenzied voice of the nightingale. Arms akimbo, I feel my muscles working on the pedals, steering with light swings of my hips—like a girl. Bah! the handlebars.

I swing off the road onto a path, past piles of hay freshly raked ready for the wagons—four pedals between each. Joy and sun and aloneness, they burst in me. I aim straight for the next big haystack, bouncing wildly over the stubble, faster, flying, straight into the sweet moist embrace. I drink deep the fermenting fumes and the world spins about, click-clicking like a bicycle wheel.

On through an uncut field, the path has disappeared, and I am careful to weave through the hay not to crush it. High ripe hay, poppies—blood-red wounds salved by the icy foam of the spittle fly—magentas of lupine and clover, lavender-brushed white buds of the wild onion—plucked, its pungent smell. The frazzling bees, the petal-fluttering of the swallowtails and whites and tigers and cloudless sulfurs and mourning cloaks. The swallow, wing drumming, slices into the grass-tip mist of insects, shooting high into the elms and above, where black feathers float on the blue, circling to skim again.

And on, through a gap in the bordering thorn thickets and broom with its yellow naga flowers, to the pine forest.

Sound turns hollow. Light presses in through the needles to take its place. Except for a twig cracking, the thud of a falling pine cone, sound is all beyond and above and in quite another space. A dog's bark hangs empty, high in the tree tops. A cuckoo, squawking as he flaps through the branches, settles somewhere with his nervous clucking, looses his sad globes of sound

—empty, outside, yet containing the whole forest.

Paths wind everywhere through the shining columns of the sun and the black columns of the pines. My bicycle finds its way, slithering sometimes on the pine needles, slowly, silently in the pollen-heavy air. And I seem emptied too, like an invisible bubble floating in the echoes.

Life is all outside. Here there is only dropping and cracking and empty hollows. The animal paths—deer and wild boar and foxes and polecats and even the hare and rabbits—hurry to escape, seeking fields and thickets and marshes and dunes. The heavy trunks bar off the vistas, the maze tightens... A chill, a dungeon chill...

1930 IFE IS frozen over, its only signs a few hurrying tracks blurred by the faint low sun, to be renewed by the moonlight. We turn into a gap in the hedge, half buried in the snow. The horse and I blow jets of steam, whipped away by the bitter sea wind.

The wind would hold us here in the land of hidden life, closing us off with sheets of snow blown from the fields, stinging, hissing around us...swept clean, stripped ...coupled. We enter the winter woods, life reverses. The wind becomes but a high reminding sound, above, behind, beyond. The forest trunks lead on into a warm and silent world. Squirrels, woodpeckers, rabbits—the blood still stings in my cheeks. My gallant charger is a gentle palfrey, snorting away the frost—startling a deer sunning in an open patch, fleeting white flag. And we are beyond their reach, forever our own time.

I am greeted by his wild crushing welcome, sweeping me off my horse and hurling me into his hidden hut, by gulps of brandy, the fire roaring in the raised fireplace—hissing of green wood for the wind would disperse any smoke today and there is no danger—the sand sizzling on the parchment window, by his brushing aside the news I had for him of his trial.

I almost think he kept the fight up on purpose—they nearly killed him—so that he'd have an excuse to go into hiding...he loves it here so. And maybe I cheered him on, though I was cowering near the door and terrified through it all. She was not pretty anyhow and he must have known how it would enrage her betrothed to dance with her like that—with the honor of a Guard's uniform to defend too, a rooster! But my friend is a savage bull! Set low, with short legs like bollards and a chest like a windlass on an ocean ship, and the men of the sea joined him and the landsmen joined the other, and from the cry "Rooster!" to uproar was an instant. Chair legs and bottles flew through the smoke and the orange glow of the oil lamps hanging from the rafters. Wine dripped onto my neck from the table where I was hiding. The windows rattled with the girls' screams of excitement and my friend's roars and the grunts and curses and crashes and the tumbling of bodies and furniture.

He loved a fight and he never quite killed or maimed anyone. So he is being tried in absentia with my father defending the empty dock.

A ham, a loaf, a bottle of brandy, two great blue cabbages and he already has a sack of potatoes—I add my booty. But all he needed was his knife, he told me …and his stories tumble out.

Those bedeviled ducks flew off this morning with the pond behind the hut frozen to their feet. His mistress the fox—the night was so cold she slipped into the hut when he had stepped out to make room for more wine, and was in bed with him till the next morning. Seagulls bring him herring already kippered for his breakfasts.

In a pause between stories, he suddenly gestures for silence. His hand slips to his side, draws out a long slender knife. With airless stealth and speed he slides soundless out the door—an instant later, the death scream of a hare. And he is back, wiping the knife on the fur, singing a bawdy song, swinging me into a jig, kissing me farewell on my lips

The sandy snowy whites of the dunes cut by a ragged shadowed path leading up toward the center—my canvas. A great tree rooted there against the silver sky, reaching leafless, branches up and out over one's head and on, lost somewhere behind where the path too began, intersected by the black coursing line of the sea beyond. Near the intersection, half-hidden by the trunk of the tree, is that a hut, a trace of smoke blowing off the chimney? Through the door, open as if to welcome someone, is a glimpse of a fire. The wind is heavy and brown with sand over all, wrinkling the snow, curling it into miniature cornices, streaming through the branches, tearing at the sea. The light forces down through the wind, from the glowing sky, from the pale sun, no brighter than a moon but with a faint warmth, and is tangled and swept along.

The forest releases me, reluctantly, closes behind. The wind has dropped with the sun. Twilight is left without dimension, without color, without weight. And we are off at a gallop, at a belly-low run. My wild stallion flies us over the frozen marsh, the dunes, the hard-packed beach where the black sea still breaks... This nag, his mind is a bucket of oats.

We race down back streets and alleys to the shed in our yard. He's at the beer-barrel trough with long sucking swallows, nostrils bubbling. No more, or you will drop with cramps or burst with the swelling oats. Rub you down with a handful of hay...it still seems wrong to sleep standing up.

To be in our town again, suddenly, shockingly, it's

like turning a painting face to the wall...Yet there are other pictures on the wall, and the room stirs softly with familiar town noises. Each picture is a window, to step in or out.

Out through my secret garden. In the half-dark, where the snow lies smooth in the shelter of the walls and holds a light of its own, where the trunks and bare branches of the fruit trees wait silently. Secret, I call it, because the garden and I, we tell each other secret things and call each other secret names. However many cousins and brothers and friends that may clatter or scuffle or crunch in the cold through this orchard and garden lot behind our house, there are always secrets that make it mine alone. A hollow in a fig trunk, a brick crumbled loose in the wall, a way the doves have of chuckling when I go by, a speck of mica in a border stone shining only at me. Always the same, always a comforting excitement.

Or back through my house. The dim musty hall, made expectant by the street noises, divides us, Father's office one side, where he will be stirring about in his dusty shelves preparing for Monday Court. And on the other, as if for me the walls were transparent, a complicated structure of lighted and dim rooms, supported against the black night by the trunk of the staircase, levels and half-levels, branching corridors, each part with its different mineness, its different time and sound and smell, its dangers and its safeties, its meanings and mysteries. Each with its bits of anger and tears and no-one-understands. Each with its guilts and confessions and forgivings. Each with its smiles and peace and excitement and reliability and unbearable impatiences. And for me, discoveries and revelations and a million leagues' distance from anyone.

On through to the final room, top of all, mine, with its pictures, its windows, its locks, its invincible bed in the darkness. A structure of people with me at the top, splendid and alone, or, if I choose, carrying my absolute power with me down into the structure. I can walk back down the corridors, into other rooms, but no one can touch me—sometimes, always, if I wish it.

I can choose now, this winter evening: The rattling cobblestones closed behind clamped shutters. The grate already lit and the lamp turned up, the pine smell of turpentine and oil, my fresh wood panels and canvas stretchers. The cold look of the jug and the basin and the sheets turned down. My pictures dim and flat and closed, leaving their lights turned down, their hearts sleeping, until that time, perhaps in the morning light, when I, or even another if I were to permit it, should wake them. My books like a hundred doors, clamoring to be thrown open, tormented, eager, sometimes I cannot choose for days which one, they seem only to stay quiet when I am painting.

Or perhaps I choose when the spring tides wash silently up the canals, rising in the marsh grasses, floating me on with light sighs and touches under a sky ringing with the thousand bells of the first invisible peepers. Or when the seagull's scream cuts the icy air over the dunes. Or when his fist swings banging down and my heart stops and blackness closes out their sneaking eyes—in pity or scorn or superiority—and the food turns to rotting wood. When my mother holds me to her and laughs gently and talks of clay feet and Icarus—and talks of a divinity. When, after years of meaningless piano routine, music flows from some hidden source through my flashing fingers. When, after nothing, with no warning and no routine and no impinging, my colors open magic windows about me.

Always there is my room. It holds me alone, it never fails me…

Do they know I'm even home yet, or will they wait for the evening test? Perhaps they sensed a draft of colder air, a change in the street sounds filtering in, but I know I avoided all the creaking planks and the squeak in the garden gate and I kept Mother's puppy from yipping at me. It is our great game, enforced with a memory of a willow-wand whipping, but rewarded with Mother's chatter and stories. The start is the dinner bell, the finish is Father's golden watch.

I sting still from the cold, my lungs ache, my heart

is trying to catch up. But I am ready. The woolly rug is warm in front of the grate. I stretch out, sketching on my sheets of newsprint. Lines loop out from a central point, like petals of a strange flower. But I have no flower in mind. What is it? Only my hand knows. Long clear loops swell out, fall back, repeat, overlapping. Shaded and blurred with specks and splinters from the bit of charcoal.

From the stairwell, looping out through the house, the dinner bell begins its summons. Quick, to be there by the seventh! Mind not to bang the doors or thump the ceilings and stairs! As I dash, I spit on my fingers, rub off the soot with the inside of my tight-stuffed pocket. Slow now, just before the dining room, to a respectful walk. We are all there, standing behind our chairs, when he comes in, tucking his gold watch back into his waistcoat.

If we start with special care, silent with the soup, elbows tightly to the side, idle hand closed and resting on the table's edge, no reaching, passing first, sitting from the hips as if the chair had no back, all the little tortures they've invented, if nerves don't get started with their snapping and buzzing and tangling from the heads of the table—then perhaps she will tell us more of her story.

I watch her from lowered eyes, not to be noticed, and wish away the electricity which can spark so and make you shiver like death—please, please, please! He is in his courtroom shadows, the candlelight is gentle, look through and see what you see. You touch your napkin to your pale lips, Mother, reach for the cameo which is always there on your breast, fingering lightly. Those are the signs. Now. How will you start? Go on, tell us, tell us about when you were little, or when we were little, or the joking professor, or the time you first left home, or when you met father, or the time you got candied apples every day for a month from the costermonger before your father found out that you had been charging them to him.

Helga

THEY ARE comically well-behaved tonight, *19* *30* and he is back in the courtroom arguing political crimes. Do they know how ill I fit this role, the placid matron mother, moderator? I who have ladled burning soup into the flower arrangement to watch them curl and wilt; who have set fire to the tufts of hair curling out of his nostrils; who, when the men have stopped the Sunday country-outing carriage to go to the side of the road to relieve themselves, have jumped out, furious at their insolence and difference, and squatted down to splash loudly beside them.

Was that my golden age, the only one I shall ever know, before the flames and furies, before they drove my parents and me out of our homeland, forced me to be foreign for the rest of my life?

Soup is a bad time to begin a story. Get it while it is hot, the quick succession of spoonfuls. But the main course—servings, cuttings, chewings, seconds, sippings, and the edge is off haste and hunger—that's the time. Now, the silent soup for sorting and selecting and drifting about in the past, in that age of certainty.

They are playing a waltz. Ooom pum pum, ooom pum pum. The tuba gurgles wetly and the drum bangs on my breastbone. The hard folding chairs, the programs with the tassels, the taste still of candied apples— the martins pick bugs from the buzz of the violins, the elms and chestnuts are breathless, gilded at the tops by the falling sun. The bandstand shines orange and white and lacy like a great fixed bonnet midst all the flutterings and ribbons and spider's-web cloth bowed about rouged and powdered cheeks. The straws and striped jackets and morning coats and the gloves pulled forever off and on. The murmurings and movings about.

Is a tea concert to be seen or heard?

High button shoes, long white stockings, my yellow velvet, pale like a lemon sorbet, pushed in at the sides by his and her thighs, all puffed on its horsehair crinoline over my furbelowed lap: that's why it's hard not to squirm.

Then there's the promenade. The winding path through the park, tea houses, the deer in their enclosure ignoring us, hating us, the poodles trotting on wooden pompon legs—they would break into tears and hysterics if they were to lose their leashes. The nods and smiles and tippings of the straws and linen caps and sometimes the full stop with the hat to the breast, the offered hand in its languid curve, the charming curtsy, but-my-how-you-have-grown-my-dear. My dear, my dear!

Blue skin and so reserved, pain and sorrow held within, refined but with cheekbones and maybe a secret slant and mystery in the eyes. Mother's are like that. Exiles, when the others have gone they will say it again and shake their heads solemnly and Maman will look at Papá gratefully and smile and hold his clumsy hand. Exiles, and the half-forgotten language with its strange angles and clicks will whisper forth, and Papá and I will be left alone for a time until they remember again and return, slow, modulated, too beautiful and exact to be real. Tea cakes in their pleated paper cups, so exquisitely decorated with flowers and clouds and birds, but all dry marzipan to the mouth.

The end—ingratitude, fire, exile. May I forget, may I find other pasts.

Shivering with excitement in the summer evening heat, sitting in my darkened room by the window— just a hint, a possible shadow, is that he? The moon shines up from the dusty street and the blue trunks of the plane trees. For a few moments, in the silence, could it be?—only a distant dog and the ring of a soldier's steel heels across the park and the barracks bugle calling the new watch. Will it come again, my enchanted song, echoing back to me from the moon—the dwindling moon through the enormous leaves, rising so late now that only he and I can embrace her? My waltz which we shall never dance now? It sings in my head and my whole heart sways to it. Faintly they touch me, two, three unconnected low whistled notes from nowhere. It is only my heart dreaming them and I shall die of despair. Let them be real, let them be real again, oh please! Let him come like a shadow again through the trees, seen and unseen, weaving on his magic bicycle to my song, whistling it ever so softly to me. Unable to end and leave and finish. And see me! See me hidden here! In the arms of the unstirring trees, reaching out to you. Do you look up, are there tears on your silver cheeks? Cry for us, my lost love, we who shall never dance or kiss or lie together.

I can feel still where your arms were about me, holding me high, so strong, high to see the tumbling clowns and the gleaming brass, the banners and garlands and pretty girls whirling in white. Tight when the great firecrackers explode and I must shut my eyes against the awful bang. I was so light then—I could have flown from your fingertip. And now I am become heavy, held numb in my shivering heart. We rushed with the crowd and wore necklaces of threaded shells and cooled our blood with icy plum juice. We bought our fortunes from a parrot, plucked from his tumbling wheel of sticks: trials and sadness, goals and gladness. We rode in a donkey carriage through the emptied back streets, high up onto the walls where the skyrockets blazed on the moonless black.

And we rode back in the narrow train, the sticky wooden benches unforgiving, the light so faint and orange, the air so thick, and you so far. My head on your shoulder, so far. Where have we been? Where did we come from? What far homes to this foreign land where we meet only in a strange new tongue?

Or: where would you take me? No one noticed—pity those who chose to doze through the drone of the evening lecture. The air was so soft wandering in the pine-pollen summer nights. Down the forest paths, balanced on your bicycle wheel, I could only sway and clutch to you and collect the fireflies' light. Fleeing the student groups, the casino—why should you be so like me, uneasy with all that? Why are we so different from them? So cautious or gentle or afraid, and you would speak to me only rudely before the others, and my smile is thin and northern. And we have the same dreams of perfection, perfection that means reserve.

You took me to the pavilion. Where the unseen river at the milldam washes away the sound of the town above. Where the band plays decorously and the mothers let their daughters dance discreetly. Where the waiters bring ices with thin wafers instead of beer. And we sat together at our little table and composed sentences to each other—how beautifully we talked and how wise we were in our new language! The waltz again and again. We dared not look into each other's eyes. How stiffly I sat, praying that you would not ask me to dance. It would hurt something, make something older that must not age, that must not be touched by us. Did you know this too?... Martins to bats, velvet to cotton, evening sun to the stars and the promise of the late moon. Let us stay, let us listen, I begged you silently.

And we stayed, and I danced with you in my heart, teasing you for stepping on my toes and whirling always in the same direction. I told you of my funny family and taught you some words of my language. Can you say them still? Will you remember? How can I smile now, as if I would hear you again?

Your ridiculous words, they are yours now—hunchbacked turkey! How could I! But perhaps you will remember and smile too, my story of the trick we played on the farmer. The farmer who had doubled the price of his turkey when my mother had admired it too much at market. "How can you tell me my price is too high! I am certainly not asking you to buy my turkey. You ask me the price, I have told you." And my brothers vowed that they would get the bird for half its worth and plotted with some friends and me. Each, casually, in turn: "A fine bird, just right for our feast day. Your price? Ah! But that is high. A beautiful bird, though. How splendid it would look on the platter. But wait! What is this! He is hunchbacked! Would you market a hunchbacked turkey! No, no, all turkeys are not hunchbacked. You would try to trick us with your country wiles! I would not have such a carcass on my table. Perhaps it is the evil eye!" Until he was so upset that he hid the turkey in a potato sack and had only artichokes for sale. We ate artichokes on feast day.

We laughed while the music waltzed and the river rushed over the dam. And were silent in the pine woods, walking your bicycle between us, afraid of each other, watching for ghosts or fairies. Past the hollow brooding barracks where echoes are stronger than sound. Through the warm smells of the bakery where the only lights burn, a lamp through the floury window, sparks from the olive twigs streaming out the chimney.

We shiver under the open sky, the fresh dew. Moonlight silvers the tops of the plane trees, the moon still hidden from us behind chimney pots. I dared hold on to you, but lightly, as we rode, slowly, winding through the tree trunks. You asked me which was my window and I showed you, alone under the gable. Would you stay until I wave? Oh do, oh do! Or we would wait, there on the bench we would sit, and say strange stiff things about each other, always using the formal address. Why could we not possess with thou? Even when you kissed me we could not say it. Lightly, trembling but with our hearts held back.

And the night when I could not meet you. Late, as

I sat here by the window listening to the night, I heard the waltz, whistled from the distance. Approaching through the streets and across the square. Finally I saw you on your bicycle, moving slowly in rhythm to your song. Soft, sad, withheld, loss. Why, even then?

Manlio

INGERING her cameo. She looks so sweet and sad and past. What have you lost, Mother? Be gay again. Tell us a story. Your grammar professor.

19 30

Helga

YOU REMEMBER how he conducted constant warfare against the peasants—cunning must *19* **30** be met with cunning—for the honor of every citizen of the town. Anything gained from a peasant is honorable. One market day, as the country people streamed into town with their wares, the professor stood at the base of the bell tower on the main street. He busied about conspicuously with sheets of paper, a long tape snaking about, craning his head back to sight up the tower, shading his eyes, muttering. Ever curious, the peasants would stop to watch him. Finally one young fellow, a bunch of chickens tied by the legs and slung over his shoulder, asked with bravado, "What are you up to, old man, not in order to know, but... It has been there a long time, that tower. It is nothing new to be taken so seriously."

"Why, I mustn't say too much, but I am on the track of something of revolutionary importance. Come, perhaps you could help me, though I don't know if your eye is clear enough, your hand steady...First I must complete the measurement of the circumference of the base here, and then I shall show you. Come around here."

The chickens were dropped in a fluttering struggling pile. The two went around the corner to the doorway of the bell tower facing on the market square.

"Hold the end of this tape just here. Keep it straight, don't move it. I shall go around carefully and come back to you on the other side."

He held the tape proudly in position. Slowly, paying out as he went, keeping it taut, the professor disappeared around the tower.

A crowd collected wondering and laughing at the strange fellow leaning so conscientiously against the bell tower on one finger. "You'll see…a very interesting discovery…not every one can do this." Waiting, waiting. Finally he called, no answer. Angry, he dropped the tape, went around the tower where he saw the other end pegged to the bricks, his chickens gone…He was too humiliated to denounce.

And the last children's party we gave—every year, on the town's feast day, all the children of the workers in Father's little factory, usually a dozen and about as many parents, in our big reception room. That year we were to put on a puppet show for them, hot drinks, cakes and candies afterwards. With the winter afternoon already almost dark, they would come in a group, all of them together. To reassure each other. Mother would look nervously at their feet, hoping there would not be too much mud tracked onto the carpet. And she would greet them all by name and be very kind. The grownups would each be given a large mug of hot wine and the children hot milk with chocolate melting in it—the carpet again. Then they would sit in a half-circle, the children on tiny chairs that Mother had had specially made for them, their backs to the great tiled oven, gleaming with its scenes of lords and ladies, heating the whole room on the wintriest day. And in front was our puppet stand.

One of the stories behind our feast day was that it honored the marriage of a princess of olden times to a great emperor and savior of our land. So our puppet show was always some invention ending in a royal wedding. This time we had a story about an impostor suitor who was really one of the local peasant lads. Stealing rich clothes, he presented himself as a foreign prince and undertook the three tests the king had required to win the princess's hand. His trick was to follow the real prince, his foremost rival, trying none of the tests himself, but, when the other had successfully completed them all, springing on him from behind a roadside hedge, cudgeling him, taking the three trophies from him—I only remember one, the dragon's tongue. He left the prince for dead and hiked off to claim the princess, proud and cocky as tomorrow's roast turkey.

But just in time, the impostor was recognized by the great crowd of peasants waiting outside the festive hall. Here we were to have an exciting scene where the crowd shouts out the fraud, dashes after their villager impostor who has taken to his heels, catches him and bears him back loyally to their beloved king for justice.

But we got no further. There was a stir in our audience, a chair banged over backwards as a man stood up, muttering fiercely, wading toward the door. Someone turned the gas up. "Damn them! They'll never change, with their patronizing…their loyal peasants… impostors, justice!…once too often!"

Children began to whimper, we cowered behind our stage. They all left, some mumbling an apology or a thanks or a "…nothing against you, nothing personal…" Most were silent.

The next day our little factory, which was just across the courtyard from our house, was barricaded against us, and by afternoon they had some kind of decree from the socialist government. Father protested and went to the courts, but every worker testified against him: abuses, rights denied. Then one night we woke to dreadful screaming and running and roaring and the smell of smoke. They must have set it, but Father knew he could not prove it—or best not. It was one wing of the house. Burned itself out without spreading. But the next day we packed up everything in two great wagons, sent them on, and took the train for the border.

And so we became exiles from our beloved country.

Manlio

PERHAPS IT IS the way he sets his fork down, or an unrhythmical dabbing with his napkin. The attention passes down the table like a half-cut cake. "At the risk of your disapproval, my dear, that was not exile. You are unexilable. You have crossed still other borders since then before finally ending here, even coming alone. Yet you have never been dispossessed. You have carried your home with you, and your convictions, wagon loads. And if you were to go back there you would find nothing remained. The exile's home is truly elsewhere and unobtainable. We shall not let you write us off so easily. Now, off with you to bed, children. Your mother will say your prayers."

We are closed in by the desolate landscape, flat, arid, dreary, so wide that motion seems hopeless—the imprisoning freedom, the tyranny of space, not even a slope, up or down, to accomplish. In the distance a range of mountains sometimes shows through the haze, but far off to the left, not on our route.

It is better to limit the outlook: the sweat dripping from my nose, my arms stretched forward to push on the tailgate with the rhythm of each step, the weathered wood, the dust lifting on the silent wheels and dropping back in puffs into the faint ruts, my knees playing their endless idiotic game of trying to hide my boots from my sight. I glance at the girl in the yellow velvet dress, not far off, pushing her cart too and, quite by chance I know, in the same direction. I do not expect her to speak, though she is my mother. I expect nothing. We both stop at the same time to rest, always the same distance apart, always silent, sound gone forever behind the horizon. The cold, with the air so dry and the sun so thin, will drive us on soon, before rest can be comfort or even change. There is no arrival, in these brief stops, no falling back and starting over. Stopping is a part of continuing. We are denied repetition.

I can see the load in her cart from all sides at once. A tiled oven sits solidly in the middle, the figures of the pattern masked with dust. A small dog, brown and sleek and brushed, rides on top. Beneath the oven—perhaps she does not see it—a kitten strangles in tangles of yarn. Tied by their yellow feet, a bunch of chickens, fouled and flapping, hangs from the tailgate. A bird cage, a door on each side, each open, is stuffed full of yellow birds struggling inwards to be at the center. Dolls and toy animals are heaped in armloads: a half-bald princess, chewed and smirched, in a gleaming ball gown; a ballerina, eyes closed, parted painted lips, naked but for one embroidered slipper; an orchestra of hedgehogs glued forever in a waltz; an elephant carved from elephant ivory; horsehair horses unable to stand; a stuffed sea-gull, its eyes missing; puppets piled together; a crocodile like a bit of painted stick. A hop vine is festooned across between the side-poles, swaying to the motion of the cart, heavy with its conical fruits.

Chains are wrapped round and round the whole pile, loosely, unsystematically, fixed with a rusty padlock on which perches a dusty buzzard painted once to be an eagle. On top of the oven, clutching to the unsteady glazed surface, is an enormous insect. It is chewing slowly, shreds of flesh hanging from its mandibles. It wears a rotted cloak cut from a flag.

Nailed askew to the side of her cart is a large mirror in an elaborately carved gold frame. Reflected in it I can see glimpses of the load on my cart, never all at once, never for more than an instant.

Around the sides of my cart, hung tight together, are my paintings, a skirt of colored paneling below the level of the open bed of the cart, reaching almost down to the dust. Fixed in place on this slowly rolling stage is a mounted church bell, its tongue swinging and jarring silently. An ax is driven into the floor, its helve, crude and shining from use, standing up at an angle, and perched on the helve a brown-white owl looking back with unblinking eyes. There's a short-handled hammer, its heavy iron head beaten at each end into deep cupped concavities, polished as smooth and soft as mercury, a stonecutter's chisel, splayed head, newly sharpened blade, a tasseled black wool shawl folded neatly, a puppy sleeping on a powdered glove, a postcard, skirts flying over a line of buttocks.

We push on.

The faint snow-capped peaks of a mountain range hang above the dust to the right now, and there is nothing to the left.

If there is any change it is a deepening of the dust. The rims of the wheels are buried now. My feet are heavier, my lungs weaker, and the sweat is caked so it can no longer flow free.

She is having great difficulty. She struggles at the spokes of the wheels or pushes with her thin shoulder to the iron reinforcements, crawling sometimes on her hands and knees. And she begins to drag things from her cart, discard them in the dust. I have not the strength to look up often, to note which pieces go first. Once or twice I look back under my arm at the line of abandoned things, lost in the dust. And I have no strength or even the wish to give her sympathy. Sympathy would be futile, soaked up in the dust before it ever could reach her.

Gradually we diverge. I can see nothing left on her cart except the rotted bit of flag, tied now to the last remaining side-post. Even the devouring insect must have been dragged off and left to twitch in her tracks. She is moving toward her own horizon now, a dwindling speck of yellow, and the flag is limp in the airless waste. She disappears.

Could I too disappear, vanish from myself into the wasteland? Can I discard it all? Would I too become barren dust? Yet the wheels bury deeper, my lungs can find no air. I can no longer go on.

On a scrap of paper which I find in one pocket, with a bit of pencil which I find in the other, I scratch a few lines, symbols, words. One for each painting and each object on the cart. And around the margins of the paper I trace the outline of the cart itself. I open a locket, still on its chain around my neck, dig out the two browned and stained photographs in it, making room for the carefully folded paper.

Unable to look back, I set off in a new direction, toward the *mountains. Without turning, I nevertheless see my cart, with all its load, settling into the distance and the dust. It disappears.*

Can the sun still rise? Can sounds return—the rooster in my secret garden, hoofs on the pavement, the single stroke of the matin bell? Can my lungs fill with winter morning air, my heart open?

Today I am to go sailing on the open sea, my first time. He has asked me. Today is a holiday. I would go if the rain were freezing to the trees, if the waves were white on a black sky, if I had to escape hungry with empty pockets and walk all the way to the port.

A clear sky just before dawn, when the stars have disappeared, can have the same flat grayness as a sky soaked with rain or frozen with snow. Now, above the gables and chimneys, it is colorless, empty of light or dark, weightless. But I can smell the snow and feel its cold dampness in the air. I can hear a wind in the rooftops, bringing the sea. Dune smells, salt, fish, seaweed, I rush into them.

The sail cracks stiff in the cold wind, the boat rides uneasy to the quay, lurching and shuddering as her master makes ready. A shout, free! Tiller down to the backward motion, sheets in, tiller up, steady! We lift into the wind and the sea.

We beat down the long channel between the breakwaters, then stand out into the open sea. Fish traps, the lighthouse, davits and masts, the chimneys of the cannery, the customs house, their stinks and clanks and flashes, shrink to minor passing intrusions on the sweep of the beach, the dark centuries of the forest, the rhythm of the hissing waves, the frozen light of the gray sky, the tumult of the driving wind.

There is ice on the shrouds, when we tack flakes fly from the sails. The sea sucks heavy on our little boat. Light fades, the sky weighs down on us. The last gull has flown off for shelter from the night and the mounting wind.

Is he afraid too? His eye is confident, he does not hesitate. And he seems unaffected by the soaking cold. We shorten sail in the shrieking twilight. Wild and uncontrolled until the storm trysail is bent on, sheeted hard as a plank. Racing off with the icy spindrift, the wind and sea on our quarter, surging, rushing on before the crest of a wave. The motion now is a swelling and lifting, caught up, torn and streaming past, then dropping back into another black trough under the wind. There, where the sea rests for a moment, where the foam driven deep beneath the surface hisses up, rides a seagull.

We rise again, veering on the steepening smooth face, high into the driving wind. And from there we can see the steady flash of the lighthouse.

✻ ✻ ✻

Fanning across my ceiling, wedges of yellow light alternate with shadow, sweeping like the message of a lighthouse through driving spray. Did I resent that lighthouse through the winter storm? How often have I come in to port since then, half-eager for comforts, hungry, half-longing to stay joined to the sea and the sky and the wind!

These lights on my ceiling, they sweep in the opposite direction to the lights passing in the street below. When I was quite young I would wonder and wonder that the sounds passing seemed to go one direction while the patterns on the ceiling would go the other. At first I suppose that I did not relate them at all. Then, it was a mystery, a delightful mystery I would carry into sleep. One night the reason came to me—I am sure I was very young. And night after night I would please myself by wondering at this strange mistake in the way things should be. It was from that solution that I made my "life camera." Experimenting, first I would close the inside shutters, leaving only a crack. The fan snapped shut, leaving a single slice of light across my ceiling, vague hints of forms in it. I studied that for nights and nights. Why the forms, what were they? I made diagrams in my notebook by flashlight—under the covers so they would not catch me. And I worked out a theory. Every night I thought about it, working out its principles. And finally it came to me, an experiment, a verification.

The next day I hurried back from school, knowing there would be full sunlight in the street for only an hour more, up to my room. I locked the door. With the leather-punch on my pocketknife, I carefully made a small hole in one of the inside shutters, in the corner of a panel by the molding to be the least noticeable. I slid my wool rug against the crack at the bottom of the door, plugged the keyhole with a bit of paper. Outside the afternoon sun was blazing full on the shops and trees and passers-by. I closed the untampered shutter tight, plugging a crack or two with paper. From the wall opposite the window I removed all the paintings, leaving a bare white expanse. Excitedly I closed the second shutter, taking care not to look back, sealing it well too. All quite ready, I turned. Extraordinary!

I still try it. Removing the carved disguising plug, or one of them—there are several now, different diameters and positions. Closing everything tight, and the world comes into my dark chamber. Faint, a little blurred, and—my triumphant proof—the images are reversed and upside down! The world, all drawn through a pinpoint, turned backwards and on its head. Walking weakly across my ceiling, trees and rooftops hanging down my wall, signs reading backwards. And I am not in it at all. It is a silent world, floating past, bent sharply in the middle. I brightened and sharpened it later by putting a lens in a larger hole—and still I have never been discovered.

Even now I need only close the shutters, let the outside bore through a single eye, spread itself before me. It will be there, dependable, much the same. Always reversed. I could paint it there from memory, a fresco in the white plaster.

ONCE...her beseeching eyes...she was with me in my room...what would a dog have with this faded twisted world? How patient she was with me, with my moving fresco, that once! A moment of curiosity, politely looking once more when I urged her, then waiting for me indulgently to finish with my foolishness, for the "Walk?" which would summon us into her world.

1950

How could I have signed for her death?

Her eyes, her imploring eyes: "Take me away, though it is too late!" Her soft, resigned, "Can I not have you back after you cruelly left me?" Dragging her half-dead body to me, hiding her face in my knees, face of fear and pain and death... Sunday-morning guns and caged live decoys in cages float across my ceiling—gallant man, useless songbird! May you blow yourselves to shreds! ...The vet's summons, the X-ray negative on the frosted panel of light, the pointing pencil: broken back, broken, kill her, kill! That is what you want. Thank you for not saying it, though, not yet...You must try, you must operate, set it. Of course, torture, little chance, but you must. We have no right to take her life.

I weep through the sunny afternoon. They must not hear my sobs and cries: weak and sentimental, too much of that, if they're in pain they must be put away, that's what they want themselves, best thing you can do for them. If this be true...but it cannot. Forgive me, forgive me! Your eyes, your beautiful free soul. You gave so much, you loved so well. My dearest friend.

Killing, that is their code, disguised. And they would persuade me. How can I stand up to their murders? The sport of kings—merciful, the natural challenge of the chase, controls the population, healthy sport. The penalty of death—justice, example, deterrent, a lesson to the community. War—because we are right, defend our way, a safe world, some things more valuable than life, because they are wrong and evil, God is on our side. Their military schools—bayonet out jab straight to the gut, twist, retrieve, jab: the discipline and precision, the clean life, to keep us strong and healthy, moral fiber, clear thinking against the fuzzy-minded and the sentimentalists, and can we afford the luxury of...The pesticides and insecticides and genocides, the vivisections and abortions and sterilizations and stamping out the messy pigeons. Walk down the line of ants and they crunch under your bare feet, spray and they curl and writhe and drop dead, cheer when the tumbrels go by, make room for the most advanced species, for the most advanced of the species, quickest and cleanest with the sledge on the back of the brain.

And they would have me kill her: merciful, painless, out of her misery, put away, put down; and you would be cruel, selfish, not to.

Yet is it true? How could she live like this? The operation has failed, I know it has, and there can be no improvement. Pain, filth, the accusing eyes. The only merciful course? Are they right? Is this different from the crippled human because the animal has no escape from pain into the intellect? Who can say that? Is this that choice where killing, though a violation of the heart, is essential? No, no! that is deception. The reason will be simple: lack of the courage to look into her eyes.

I am so tired. Where must I go? You fight for your life with every force of your heart, yet even I, your one hope, with the power of God, consider your death. You are deserted, as you knew from the beginning.

M **19 30** Y TIME-KEEPER is this upside-down world of mine. Now it glows brightest with the late afternoon sun, the shadowy figures stroll, only a few hurrying, winding among the others. Or there is the pale motionless scene of the early morning, the street lights are my gloomy chandeliers. Or the faded mid-morning when the lull is given its tempo by the street sweeper working slowly down the opposite gutter.

I have learned enough now. No longer do I go to the window to check, to identify some filmy event or character on my screen. It is too brutal. Wrenched around, turned over, the blow striking into my brain from the untempered light, I'm confused into too many dimensions, and must endure the irksome wait afterwards until the jangle calms and my eyes regain their perception. I know what is out there. Now I am free to design as I will.

I see from my time-keeper that it is late afternoon. Have I slept? This tender languor, enfeebling, this half-death—is it sleep's release, despair? She is dead now, I am certain—the signal is clear as death, shriek in a forest night. My execution order has been carried out— they even made me do that, in writing so there would be no mistake. Despair seeps out, remorse, until my heart seems drained away. I have killed her. I have no strength for tears.

The scene passes on across my ceiling, along my empty wall.

Awareness flows out through me, restlessness stirs.

The house will be quiet now, no one moving about.

I escape. To the secret garden, the back streets where no one is likely to break in on me; to the fields of yellowing grain beyond the walls of the town, where still some sun slants in; to the bank of the feeder canal where I keep my skiff chained to a poplar tree. Unplanned, unthinking, almost unaware, for I see only her, dashing after butterflies, leaping on me, far ahead waiting impatiently, bounding in the weeds on the scent of chickens' nests. The pole and paddle are there where I hide them in the rushes—except during the winter floods and spring tides. Flat-bottomed, narrow, an ugly exaggerated sheer, splotched with mud—it is not much in itself, no bird of the sea. But it can carry me—and she would come too, riding proudly in the bow—deep into the marshes, down canals and ditches in the reeds, into the lagoons behind the dunes, where no one ever goes. Where life changes by seasons but not by years. Where the ancients lived on anchored rafts and platforms and sent their dead drifting in skiffs like this, drifting down the inlets on the offshore breeze, out onto the rolling sea.

In the twilight, we slip quietly through the grasses, frogs plopping ahead or not bothering, bats competing with the shrilling swifts and martins, the sky glowing yellow, dew in the air while the sun is still on the distant pines, the scops owl and the nightingale sounding the evening while the hoopoe and cuckoo and the mourning dove still call mournfully to the dying day.

I am at the willow stump. I step out softly, not to disturb the voices of the evening, on round the stuccoed walls to the cemetery's gate off the country path. Here the light is fainter, chiller. The faded wraiths and withering flowers in their little tubes are darkening. Father's grave stands white and sharp and new in the packed earth. The councilors' floral wreath with its patriotic ribbons lies heavily on the marble. My sprig from the flowering laurel tree covers the date of his death.

Why must I know him only now, love him too late? He is gone, with his punctualities and disciplines, the hand banging like a gavel on the table, his endless "critical times" when the rule of silence was absolute, his public defenses practiced on us with such passion. His great bony figure, stooped and weary, that paced up and down, searching for some impossible best. His face furrowed deep, eyes hidden black beneath the shocks of his eyebrows—but ready to smile on us with a breath-taking generosity. Respect, patience, but final inflexible judgment, his awesome rightness.

How could such a man have tolerated me, have managed always to give me full respect—with my violations and vagaries, my different choices, the heavy smell of my paints everywhere? My irrationalities, my rough friends, my wanderings in wild places so alien to him, my dreams and collections and useless ideas?

And no one else could have controlled and removed the harm from mother's stinging prejudices and intolerances, borne her stubbornnesses and coaxed them into smiles. Yet I think he made no adjustments. Intolerances? Yes, but based on a code so rigorous and complete that it always wore the robes of justice, a permanent justice which admitted no change. Everything about him was fixed and certain and permanent and reliable. And now he is dead.

It is dark enough now to see the male fireflies exploring the moist evening air, and in the grass, earthbound, the wingless glowing females. Is this the way of it? For all his fixity, was he the one who could fly, while she is weighted to the earth?

The sun has set, leaving only its flaming memory against the purple sky. I return on silent waters.

M Y BRAIN IS A wound, ripped by the *19 42* flying steel of this ugly war. Just beyond this twisted beam of the station ceiling I see him, writhing in the settling dust and flies, in the litter accumulated during the weeks of siege. I see the silent screams in the roar of explosions and machines and falling rubble. Who lies there kicking and stamping the heavy air? Oh help him, he must have help!—he so near I can see the nerves curling back into the flesh. I, pinned absurdly by the legs. Some one has come, kneeling quickly over him, inspecting. . .morphine, for God's sake, even if he is to die!. . .furtively, searching the pockets, wrenching in the mouth. In that shocked moment something in me bursts open like a mouse in a bell jar, white, pink, then the rush of red. In that moment, with every thread of my will, I fire my service pistol—three, four shots. The figure flees, dives into the smoking ruins.

My tears roll into the dust and lie still. He too lies still, his wound blackening, his jaw dangling, his eyes staring at me in horror. I heave up as high as I can on one arm and hurl the pistol into the ruins.

They say I am unhurt. The blood was his. It had spread out slowly until its furthest limit had reached me, stuck drying to my cheek, to my officer's tunic, as I lay there sobbing.

I am released. The air is hazy and brilliant about me. I can hardly feel my weight. The pavement is soft and uncertain, it has lost its usual force, its pressure against my feet. The dust is foam on a changing undecided sea. In the clamor of the ambulances—vague figures hurrying, hurrying aimlessly—I simply go. No one stops me, no one cares, no one knows. At each step the ground drops away, never coming up to meet me. My arms are my sails to pull me forward, righting me on this curving sea where the horizon slips by so fast.

Somehow I find the bus station.

Burned abandoned countryside works its joggling way past my smeared window. My stomach rides in my skull, sloshing against my temples, pulsating like a limpid jellyfish. I shiver convulsively in the heat. The bus smells of chickens, dung, vomit, synthetic tobacco, sweat, sweet fresh bread in a burlap bag by the driver's seat, new-dug onions, woman's heat. I sort these all out by memory, reaching back and back, for to the eye we are only the driver, the bread, and I—and his Beretta pistol, swinging loosely from his belt in its green leather holster, swinging merrily.

My clothes are filthy. They are not my own. From where and whom? How did I get here? And my uniform—did I get rid of it completely, its identity? My uniform! Those days of patriotism when that was the easy way, the adventure, no questions. The swing, the excitement, and I am so handsome. I march across my ceiling, smartest of all—both seeing and being seen, how extraordinary! The sun glints on my buttons. Already I have a medal for target shooting. Command and be commanded, it is so splendid.

Where did delusion begin? When did time become heavy with its nothingness? Father could have told me, but he was already dead. Mother? No, for her it was only pride and danger, smiles and tears. Danger meant nothing, and she could tell me nothing of killing and brutality. "Ah, how romantic, I lose a boy, he returns a man"—or a telegram or a medal. Who was there to tell me that I, I myself, must kill? It was always someone else, some other unit, some other front. We were liberators by another's victory, we retreated at another's loss.

More medals, that's how they dealt with doubt, while the machinery of patriotism ran down, while the polish wore off—while their war was being lost. They proclaimed supreme efforts and clear calls, sacrifices and greater glories, common causes—and the crushing, the stamping out. Pips and stripes ruled while governments scrambled and scrabbled for loot, and heroism became absurd.

My dreadful heroism.

I was front-line inspecting for one of their rear-echelon bureaucracies. I saw a rifleman shot in the thigh, blood spurting. I snaked to him and got him back to the medics. Minutes later his ambulance was blown to bits—spread out over a field of grain—by his own battery...And they ask forgiveness, and blessings.

But now, where am I going? How could there be an empty bus? It must be heading away from the city—I daren't ask the driver. Have I paid? Does he know? My head seems less liquid, riding without support, carrying its messy contents better. The countryside is negative, rejecting us. But in the distance, through the hair oil, the sticky fingers, the tufts of chicken down, are mountains. We have left the main road and are heading toward them.

Shall I hear the echo of shots even from there? The pistol swings and swings, a child's toy hanging over the cradle. What holds me here as if I were crucified to the sticky leather? Why must that orange fly-specked light burn down on me, only me, over my seat, though there is bright daylight beyond the strip of windows? What do they know, what is there to know, who are they? Let me break through this glass, give me back my strength! I shall go back, I shall find the pistol and those eyes and the other with his pockets stuffed with gold and crumpled notes. Let me be free! You cannot carry me off this way, without proof, without a trial, a court-martial, without witnesses, without the honor of uniform. I'll not let you kill me, you will not catch me and drag me out and shoot holes into my bursting skull! I am the one that can kill.

I am the one that can kill. Her bones, his putrid corpse. And the long unbroken space of the past. "Your duty…merciful…martial law…" But the horror in the eyes and the blood from the dangling jaw…and did my bullets hit the other, is he dead? He did not stop or wince or scream. Who saw, who knows—when I do not know myself? But from the moment he was wrenching at the teeth—the rifled money, I reaching painfully for my gun, four careful shots—until I was lying broken, I wanted to kill. With every force of my heart I wanted to kill.

Can any part of innocence survive?

Even now I can stand in my secret garden in the night, look up and see our house as a skeleton, as if the walls were stripped away, leaving its glowing yellow limbs about the central column, look into my room with its shadowy upside-down world wrapped about me, protecting me.

Or I can reach into unbroken stretches of dunes and forests and lagoons. Or there's my horde of se-crets: paths, back waterways, hidden places in the gar-den where the psychic currents were so strong, certain books in father's library which have coded messages only for me, cracks in the plaster giving mystic signs, pictures in the museum which know me when I come to visit, my own paintings which sometimes speak to me in whispers of magical places and unendurable loves. The unbearable sweetness of spun-sugar balls on their colored sticks. The cool sand at the edge of the tide, the perfumed smoke at sunset rising in white columns from each farmer's cottage, great bundles of fruit-tree prunings to boil the soup and give warmth against the night's frost.

But I wanted to kill, I killed. Crumbled away, shards covered over by the sifting dust.

We continue on, up into the hills.

**19
47** "Y DEAR, you know, I like talking to you so much. You say such unusual things. And you work so hard. Why, just think what it means that you would talk with the likes of me at all! What was it you said last cocktail party to me? That a writer must die, simply die, before he can write. Of course, I don't think you're right at all. I've known many very famous writers who are quite lively. In fact, I suspect you are too. And you're just trying to shock me. I wish my husband were just a tiny bit like you."

"No, no! It's true. A writer is so removed from life, looking back on life as he writes, his vantage point is so God-like, that it must in a way be death."

"But don't you think one must live life, really live right in the middle of it, before one can be so presumptuous as to tell other people about it? But it must be so exciting, with your new book almost finished! Giving birth to your baby, no?"

"It is not a baby to me. It's in its old age. I kill it when I finish it. Let it join the other ghosts. I shall never see it again. Shouldn't want to."

"But there you go again! Death, killing. Always like this..." she draws the corners of her lovely painted mouth down around her dimpled chin with her thumb and forefinger, salmon-gloved, "...aren't we? But you are so amusing. I like writers. Isn't he adorable, dear?"

≠233≒

You turn your golden head just a fraction toward me, your sapphire eyes swing carefully to their mascaraed corners, for an instant only, to make sure of me. Why do you loathe me so? Did you marry me so that you could enjoy loathing me at cocktail parties? You were so enchanted by my medals.

But you have never killed. You have never ridden off with a busload of ghosts into the mountains, leaving behind ruins and eyes of horror, and come back with nothing but medals to find the world missing.

I did not try to return. That is what you wanted too, was it not? Except, of course, how could you know what return means? I do what your father wants of me, presentably. I am quite in this world of yours. It is only that I do not understand it, I can no longer breathe deeply.

Am I like your simpering writer? Do I look from the vantage point of death? I keep it to myself, I tell no one. Stifled, yet I let you marry me. Voiceless, yet I let myself answer and agree. You line my life with mirrors. Your asides to me, your negative questions, they are reflections of what things are, or perhaps are not. Your staging, it puts me always in contrast. Your hints and corrections and silences. Sometimes I think you direct an entire cocktail party, and play a principal role in it, all with the end of displaying my humiliation.

You have several methods. You lead me carefully through the crowds, introducing me, leaving me nothing to say. Or you force me to simper, you drag innu-endoes from me, you raise blushes and denials and then laugh as if I were a performing poodle. Or you leave me, and the entire room turns away as if I did not exist. I would escape then but I do not have the cour-age to face a late arrival coming in at just that moment, or the wave of laughter through the still open door to your "Isn't he too sweet! So unspoiled! And I simply can't get his clothes to hang right!" and the echoes "...mad romantic...nature boy...her breeding stock..."

My old paintings, they amuse you—they line our walls, windows looking in on me blankly. It is you that mock, not they. They are silent, having nothing to say to me now and never having known your language. And the shelves of books, all carefully cut, untouched except for dusting. The perfumes in their bottles, to be used according to plan—Pine, Wild Flowers, Anguish, Sea Breeze, Passion, Heartache, Ecstasy, Mystery, Nights of Love. Photographs of your father's yacht—me, in white ducks and the anchor-pattern sweater and the cap, being handed on board by a sailor with the face of an ancient mariner. You, lying on the deck, your body exposed, someone rubbing oil on your thigh, a gull soaring over the bowsprit. Your calendar, appropriately circled, the cabinet of preparations and devices lightly dusted with lilac powder, the door between us with its humiliating signals.

Mirrors, pictures—reflections, they circle me endlessly, their gestures and laughter, their clever mockery, their inescapable glare. They gleam through me, back and forth, until I am canceled and they have achieved their purpose and they continue heedless. Why did they ever take the trouble? Or was it no trouble, but only the natural properties of their glassy surfaces?

But something has been left of me, else why should I continue apart, why can I curse them, why do I rip at her hateful calendar, turn my pictures to the wall, feel still the passion of shame?

I shall go, I know that now. They will not miss me, they are a closed system, without interactions or unaccounted-for elements, accelerating, but entirely predictable. And by their acceleration they are doomed. I am waiting for a sign, that is all, something to show me the path.

IF I COULD, if I had ever believed, I would pray now. I would set loose my silent cry of thanks. For I hear the high wild scream calling to me. I have run through the night, alone under the wind, streaming through the phosphorescence, thrown wildly in the waves. To this impossible dawn, spreading the horizon out around me, showing me a world I thought I would never find again, embracing me... Racing on with the foam hissing behind, yawing in great surges as waves pass on, licking the belly of the sail...From escape to discovery...A bit of bread to tear at, from the fishermen of Ravenna where I bought my boat. The squint returned to my eyes, the salt in my beard, the pulse of the sea in my muscles. The grip of the sea on the tiller, her lift and swing and recovery, the music of the water running beneath her graceful forefoot. Her strong mast swinging against the stormy sky, urging us on under the sweep of dark canvas. Now, with the exhilaration of past despair, I could ride with her down the last purple wave, cleave into the healing forgiving deep.

The keel drives up onto the shingle, the sail drops wildly. With tackle fastened through a great hole etched in a granite boulder, I warp up out of the tide, grinding in the sand. The rainstorm which has been chasing me breaks against the headland, drenches me in an instant. I dive into a cave carved in the limestone by the winter waves and driven sands. A flock of sheep streams in to join me, followed by a figure in a conical hooded cape smelling pleasantly of wet goats' wool. Silently, together, we make a fire of driftwood. Our shadows dance to the howl of the wind.

He is my friend now, this shepherd of Gargano. Even then, back in our cave, he could understand why I had come to his land. As we talked to the music of the storm, sharing my bread and his milk and cheese, he took his pruning knife from the horn sheath at his braided horsehair belt, honed it on his palm, began carving intricate patterns in a cork-oak chunk. I asked him where he found his designs, he thought for a time, he answered.

"I walk after my sheep. I have a piece of wood and my knife. And I have got an idea. However, it isn't clear. So I begin to carve. And then the idea becomes clear while I work."

I have started again, through him and through you, my love.

Did you see my bit of sail, racing sun-white still before the storm, did you wonder whether the waves had swallowed me, or did you know I'd be there when you came down to the beach, the sun shining on your dripping dark hair as you stepped carefully through the line of sheep, were you waiting too?

You too rejected, lost, suffering the guilt of your marriage. Fled to this unreached world where idle dreams are burned away by the sun, where the skeleton of the land is bare and tempered to resist, where there is room for hunger and love, where beauty and the harshness of time lie together.

We have lain under the sun, where the tide is caught in the sand, a pool sheltered by defiant cliffs and the dunes thrown up from the sea. We have loved under the wind, deep to the single soul, enfolded and enfolding our hope.

Your head is on my breast. Weeping softly, you whisper, "But it is no longer young..." Accept, my love, continue, there is no return.

We speak through silence.

I paint and my paintings are stripped clean, bleached by the sun, swept by the wind from the sea. No return, no light heart, no careless gesture.

Bones and muscle, the eternal and the proud. You naked on the canvas, you become the landscape, austere, honest, calm.

It is feast day, though not for the sheep—depleted by two turning on a spit, driven off to stay for the whole day and night in a narrow pen, or a cave fenced with piled-up thorn bushes, or, if they're in the high summer pastures or on the long drive up there, under a great rope net where they bleat and seethe for a time and then lie quiet. For our friend it is the day to return to his birthplace. He would have us join him.

We ask him why he would take us there.

"There is something there for us."

We have come on ponies, up through the throbbing slivered shade of the pines, through heavy chestnut forests, moist even now where the hills soak the mist from the south winds. Into the high valleys where the brooks still fall over the white stone, to disappear before they reach the sea and to be found again only with heavy buckets swung from deep wells on counterbalanced cranes. Up where the beech and the spruce mix. Where men, a few left, still live in the skins of beasts, on the bounty of the forests, speak an intricate archaic language. By the selective process of defiance, the weak disappearing down the long paths to the north and to the cities, those remaining are proud and fierce and scornful more than ever. Yet their eyes are soft.

Up to the highlands, where the wind and the scouring rains and sleets and snows permit only grasses and heather and gorse and prickly pear. In a hollow where there is some protection, guarded by huge boulders, stands his silent home. Here, when wool was prized, was an ancient sheep ranch, no longer able to survive the changing appetites and the factories' flood.

A home, sheltering and protecting and encouraging, containing through the generations. Such is this, however ravaged and apparently abandoned.

The walls are an arm span thick. They buttress out to hold the roof of vaulted stone. The floors are the mountain itself, rock chipped level, ground and worn smooth. The windows are gone, the doors broken loose, charred sticks and ashes are scattered on the floor, blown out of the great hooded fireplace. Through the empty openings, dazzling in the thin white air, the few dying fruit trees struggle in the wind, the weeds in the vegetable garden fling wildly, spread their seed amongst the ancient grape vines.

He tips the last of his sweet wine from a black oaken cask, cloudy, dregs slowly sinking, sweet from the summer suns of long ago. Hands us little glasses. Bits of cold mutton, bread. The sign of the cross.

Later, I come upon him in a small room behind the chimney—perhaps the room where he was born. He is sitting in the window, on its wide ledge, framed by the hewn stone. His head turned, he seems to be looking out over the pasture lands, out where the clouds form far below and stream past the mountain's flanks, beyond, across the lower hills, the plain, the sea, to that furthest reach where all dissolves. Yet there is a sense of the concentration of his thoughts back and inward to this room, a force from his eye and his heart intent on communion with the spirit of his home. The room is almost empty: a few bits of broken dusty furniture, a chipped enamel pot, a torn picture of a praying mother and child hanging by one corner on the stained plaster, stirring in the wind, a discarded walking stick, worn and frayed at the tip, carved with an intricate design of diamond shapes. Yet it is crowded. Strong and alive and free, filled with the force to endure. Vibrating, sparking with the energies of mystery.

I would not interrupt him, intrude on this reunion of ghosts. I stand in the doorway. Just inside, almost at my hand, is a small table of woven willow and cane, the legs of fruit wood carved with crescent and lozenge patterns. It is delicate, beautifully designed. I cannot tell its use—perhaps for objects of remembrance, for a flowering branch in a glass jar, a shining crystal of fool's gold, a tin of precious salt. The Penates of this home.

With no will from me, my hand reaches out over this table, as if to caress its beauty or touch an unseen object lying on it. Suspended, a thumb's length above its dusty surface. I cannot or would not move. I stare, calmly, I cannot say for how long. My vision narrows, the table fills my perceptions. It stirs, swaying in the bright air, rises firmly to my hand. The touch of its webbed surface brings back my will. I lower it, with difficulty withdraw my hand.

I 9 5 2 HAVE COME to pay the price, to buy a bit of rock with a ruin of an ancient watchtower on it hanging over the sea, to buy our right to remain in this ancient land. Yet am I hanging back, is there something I should have known?

The price: The stinks, the clamor, the blotting of the light and sky. Permissions and concessions and agreements…be solicitous to their bureaucracy, be scornful of that poor land as the only thing left that you can afford, and they will grant it to you, suspecting nothing. You need never revisit them. Walk on, they will be expecting you.

City heat fouls me as I walk, sticky, greasy, out into the wilderness of new blocks where nothing grows, where no irregularity eases the eye, where the din of motors and loudspeakers is reflected geometrically. Where all petty officials aspire to live. It is a purposeful contrast, some great design has made it so, to give me humility before the gift I am being given, to charge me with penance.

The lobby echoes, lifeless, to my nailed boots. Machinery whirs to swing the doors closed, to open the elevator, to play unmusic in my brain as I rise in this aluminum casket up through the layers of filed dwellers. I'm dismissed to a narrow corridor, the ceiling pressing down on me. I'm isolated by thin crusts of bricks and plaster, trapped. They have lured me so easily. For all my wariness and resistance I am at the mercy of their flimsy constructions, their deadly constructions.

I touch the button, chimes sound, I enter. "Would you wait a moment? He'll be right there." The room is objects. To the throb of the air conditioner rattling in the thin wall under the window, the air weakened, filtered with the stale stinks of ozone and tobacco, of sweat seeping through the deodorizers, I undertake an inspection.

A red light rotates under cardboard logs in the moveable fireplace. Everything else is motionless. The furniture is flow-shaped, veneered, glistening, spindly. Glass tops in the tables are cut in formless shapes like cat puddles on a waxed floor, chairs buttock-shaped, vented. Then the memorabilia, the decorative objects, cluttered everywhere—in glass cabinets just for the purpose, on every table, hanging from the lights, stuck at staggered levels to the walls, standing ready in every corner, on the moveable mantelpiece. Plastic flowers, ceramic vases gilded machine-oil iridescent, hollow tree trunks. A stretched-neck china cat with a sophisticated look. An enormous brandy snifter. A duck dressed like an admiral, playing a violin. Lamps copying oriental copies of occidental candle stands. Straw figures of beetles playing band instruments. A miniature copy of a peasant's water jug. A machine-stamped iron rack of dusty plastic fruit. A black plastic Negro baby with brass rings in its ears. Hooked to the walls, plates that could not be plates, impossible shapes with lumpy high reliefs of costumed country girls.

The window, slitted with its regulation blind, looks out over a wasteland of foundations and construction, flood-lit for the night shift. There is no sky.

Energetic, cool, informal, preferring the professional

to the official: "There you are. Glad you could come. Thought you would be interested, in connection with your application to purchase, of course, and as a university man from my own faculty—yes, we know something about you. Unofficially, of course, take a look at something the Council approved just today. That's why I asked you around. If you'll sit here...coffee?...I'll unroll these plans for you."

To the sucking of the air conditioner, the shudder and roar of the engines outside, the crackling of his plans and blueprints: "You're in on a good thing. Of course, you know, you'll have to raise your bid, but it will be worth it to you."

Odd to see one's feet through a table, worn nailed boots on his plastic tiles. His map slides over them. Use-zones are blocked in in color, the sea is a hasty blue. Roads, with their gradients and radius curves, lead to the heart: multi-family, recreation, swimming pools, community centers, sewage, parking, galleries, outlooks, strips, concessions, scenic cable ways, panoramic littorals.

Their Penates.

What can I tell you, my dearest? How can I return to you? By the cliffs and dunes where you wait, where the sinews of the land loosen, let go—there I must lie with you again and tell you of the truth... I wanted to kill, nothing else matters. Three, four, hammering against my shoulder, careful. Eyes of horror, a figure disappearing in the ruins...The illusion that we belonged and that the others did not. We, the first, the instrument. The illusion that the one could be separated from the many, that we need not share the guilt... Retreat, however hopeless—or the silent descent.

Y OU STILL LIE in your plot, Father. They have not moved you yet to make room, 19 97 piled your bones down in the crypt to mix with your ancestors. The marble is stained now, melted by the acid air. There are no wreaths or flowers, and I have none for you—none grow here now. But I honor you, though I do not know how to pray, I embrace you, and your neighbors too, I know some of them, your friends. You are fortunate to be here, to have your walls built around you, high, to have your hallowed ground—it is still respected.

You must know, though, that there are always fewer in whom you may relive. The cycles are drawing to a close. Immortality, if that is what it is, approaches its end...*Extinctus*...

Extinctus, written neatly, gold lettering, on the closing door...my recurring dream. We have feasted together as affectionate friends, not separated by years but by wisdom and fortune. We rise from the banquet table, crowded with our family and friends. We go out together, talking quietly. In the anteroom we are alone. A blank door leads off. "Will you take this opportunity? Will you join me?" I decline, you pass through. And now, as the door closes, the lettering appears. *Extinctus.*

From where you lie you can see only cypresses pointing into your square patch of sky. You knew what lay beyond, the fields and vineyards, the canals and paths, the far wall of the pine forest, the voices of the birds and the wind. All that is gone, even the night. Orange flame flares from a dozen stacks, burning the sky, discarding the earth's substance. Steel towers and tanks surround you, pipes wind through the air, sheds and warehouses stretch as far as the eye can see. The blue lights of welding, the steel hammering of riveters, engines roaring to accelerate, the steady grinding of conveyors, and men climbing through it all, weaving about in trucks, in little carts.

You would recognize it, Father, you would know what it is. But you would not understand the proportion. No one can. No one is responsible, few care. But it would be obvious to you that at some recent time there was a deforming, a dreadful corruption.

This is what I must tell you. So that you will know where we have gone, what has become of our love, why the life that remains is within these walls, not beyond.

But let me try to tell you more. We have time, you and I. Let me tell you something of my search and my retreat. They will come for me, but not for a while yet. And perhaps, even when they do, I shall find new life.

Once, the sea had borne me from them, far, and I had found an old land which they could not want, which was beyond their reach. There I found a woman. She too had escaped. And we joined and became man and wife. There I found a friend. He took us to his ancestors. We were content. It was a land of strong light and unceasing wind, of pain and truth, of heavy work, of contact with the earth. There was nothing ugly there, no understanding of ugliness. And, as it turned out, no defense against it. For they came, they found us. Perhaps, even, we showed them the way— and that is the greatest curse of all. My friend perished. They drove us on.

We found other lands and ways, sometimes found joy and hope.

We searched deep into the hills. With all the coasts to despoil they would not be interested in the back country. We came upon a valley, high in the hills, an abandoned house of stone, land we could work, an uninterrupted view of the mountain peaks, a few people left, holding fiercely to the soil. The nearest house, twenty minutes' walk away, was occupied. I went to call before deciding. A poet, they said, not from these parts but moved here years ago. A survivor?

Through cobwebs, the low vaulted ceilings weighing down, up dim stone stairs, he led me to his study, a tower room, I should guess, though all the windows were boarded shut—against the winter, he said. It was crowded: a tattered red plush sofa, gold-framed fading photographs of his past borrowed splendor, autographed bits of verse, books to one side under layers of dust, black flowers pressed behind glass. On a teetering table were his plans and projects—roads, villas, shops—spread out in disorderly piles, dirty with work.

We tried the city too. To its oldest center, where there could be no room left for progress, where those who chose to stay might be survivors. There was a courtyard of our own where we could grow flowers and vegetables. For a time it seemed to be going well. My painting continued. My dear wife posed for me day after day, patiently, beautifully... If only you could have seen her before she went away.

Yet each hope withered.

Our garden began to grow, but the plants were unhealthy for want of sun, dull with the grease and dust and poisons that settled on them. The din of the city flooded over the high surrounding building, loudspeakers to which we had no reply attacked us from the dwelling looking onto the courtyard.

The heart of the city was much in demand—status. There was an everlasting climbing all about us, a vying, a tangle of comparisons, waves of fads and cultism swept through, drowning everything. I could sell no paintings. I was out of phase, and no one bought paintings because they might like them. No one knew how to like.

We were driven on.

Once we found an island and on its far shore a remoteness that gave us hope. The air was still clean and brilliant. High on the cliffs we would lie together, the wind would rush on and on and there seemed no end. The hawks would watch over us. Swimming, lying naked in the sea moss with the waves foaming over. Climbing up to the pines, hot in the chant of the cicadas. Cooled in the shade, facing the soft haze of the west wind, perfumed with the resins and honey of the bush. Waves of the sweet air, the cicadas winding out their death.

Sweet dying...

No, no, I need not go yet. Will you let me stay? I am tired, a little faint from hunger. Let me rest with you yet a while. You always sought the truth. Let me tell you mine. Our ways divided once. You chose justice, I chose freedom. The one excludes the other, we both knew that. But neither of us has found his way, not for more than a few moments of great joy. So let me sit here with you, Father, tell you of our lost hopes and warn you of the end.

Once again we sought our retreat in the sea. I had been building a boat on a new design of my own, slowly and with great care, working first on paper, then with half-scale models. It was satisfying work, absorbing my thoughts, employing the skills of my hands and the theories in my brain.

I finally finished. We launched her. We outfitted and provisioned adequately for several months.

The first day at sea I was busy with many small adjustments, learning how best to handle the radical rig—the sail was such that several of my instinctive reactions had to be reversed. And I had decided to add a small motor; it needed much attention.

On the first night watch, though, she sleeping in the little cabin…how can I tell you if you have never been to sea?

A night at sea. There is no greater solitude, no greater harmony. You are confronted by the edge of the world, by the terror of the unknown, close about you in the darkness. Your self is the center and the limit, washed clean and bare, limpid, entirely within reach. The unfathomable voice of the sea through the night, the inexpressible distance of the star, the giving and the taking back, traceless.

And dawn does come, slowly, a kind of wakening of the darkness. When the sky reappears it is so colorless that you cannot tell overcast from cloudless, and with it comes torpor in the spirit and the motion and the forward flow, a pause between night and day, everything postponed. The trance lifts with the full light and the gathering of the wind.

She sleeps on below. It is better, I shall let her. I need time to understand.

Working into my awareness for some hours now has been the peculiar motion of the boat. A good sea has been running off the quarter and a steady wind. But we have not been rising quickly to the thrust of the waves. I begin to test this on different points of sailing. And I learn that my boat will fail in a heavy sea. I know this, I know it surely, and I do not avoid it as one might a lesser failure. It means the end of plans for ocean voyaging. Coastwise, fair weather, only.

I have changed course, heading for that same lost land, for its torn and ravaged shores. The wind has come in faintly from the south, brown and dank. The sea is an all-over sullen gray, swelling in restless lumps, unpleasantly. We roll on fitfully, the sails slacking and filling, the boom tossing and slamming in its tackle. The undecided waves are slick with oil and sometimes crusted with filthy scabs of tar. The white bellies of dead fish, float slowly by, deserted by the seagulls. Even the sounds of the sea have become distorted, exaggerated... The roar of whispered sounds in my bursting head, my dry breathing, the waves of blood in the sand of my brain. The sheets so hot, the sun slicing a yellow slit in the shutter. I shall crack open and spill forth poison. Leave me be!—But we need the bed, you are not hurt; quietly now, out through that door—Where, where? Can't you see the blood on me, smell the poison! Escape! Into the ruins... The motor drives rivets in the metal sea, adding its stink and scum, jiggling us like masturbating idiots into the fetid wind.

O Father, forgive me if I sink too far into my story. Should I curse memory, for often I have? What use is it if it only drives me finally back into the ruins? Yet I cannot escape it, it will not be stilled. And I have promised to show you the truth.

With the sea killed too I had no hope left of finding an uncorrupted domain. Hopeless, yet we continued, though on a lesser search, for now the most we could expect could be only a moment of relief, a passing exhilaration, a pause as the circle drew tighter.

We were not always alone. Sometimes we glimpsed others who still survived. Usually they were hurrying in different directions. And we were wary of exposing ourselves, distrustful. There were periods when it became fashionable to search, or to appear to search—

fake rebellions, pre-packaged with instructions. And we were jealous of our discoveries, however petty.

More than once we came upon evidence of survivors who had sought to wall themselves off from destruction. Their fates were various. Law could flood over them like the mounting waters behind a dam. Entry could be gained under the disguise of fellow survivors. I have seen skeletons clutching to the tops of walls—expiring in a last effort to raise still another course of masonry, or seeking escape from starvation of the body or soul, or standing final lookout for the enemy, or screaming the last curse. Enclaves. Doomed if only because they were there, obstructions in the path of progress. Doomed by the suck of their inner vacuum. Walls built higher and higher, the sky from within receding to a distant hole in the blackness, the air thick and deadly. Finally closing in, collapsing.

My paintings sold only rarely now. I believed, though my wife would not agree, that the authorities were managing this deliberately, rationing me so tightly that I would be forced to quit my retreat and my rebellion, join their ranks, and paint as they would have me paint. We were driven to living under difficult conditions. Moving often, having to stay near their centers in order to get enough sales to live on, unable to afford either the permanence of an enclave or the distance of whatever deserts still remained. Their organization was such that it was almost impossible to avoid the appurtenances of their civilization. And yet we could not support them, and did not want them—the drudgery of their machines, the nervous toil, the dependence, the poisoned products, the waste, the destruction. Try as we would we could not live without their money.

For a time I was forced to work for them, painting propaganda for travel. They had the notion that everyone should visit and know everyone else, eliminating misunderstanding, eventually doing away with all differences between peoples. They caught me, however, deliberately avoiding mention of certain areas that I had some dream of saving. I was dismissed. Thereafter I sold even fewer paintings.

My dear wife…our life together was approaching its end.

That last day had its portents: the dry light-headed air of early morning which foretells a change in the wind, air so thin that outside sounds click off into space unsustained, inner sounds crackling with static, and a high singing and a cloudless darkening—locusts gathering in the upper air. And the scraps, the rind of a bit of cheese, that I put out every night for a neighboring hedgehog, were untouched in the bowl.

That morning I put the final touches on her painting. She poses for it serenely—her lovely black hair, it can reach to her thighs when she throws her head back, her glowing olive skin, her body so light, wasted, like the morning air. This is no time for luxurious flesh, soft and meant only for the unearned cream of love. I see to her heart too, its gravity, its sadness, and its enduring joy. Yes, joy there too. Bits of memory, moments caught from dreams, signs and secret language from our life together, giving that joy to her, here.

Why do I linger over it now though? It is finished. Let me take it to her. It will cheer her to see it. Surely the high droning and the hollowness of the air have come to her too and in her weakened state may work distressingly on her.

She does not see me at first, lying flat on our hard pallet, staring up at the beams. The air is different here, there is a suspension and an absolute stillness, as if a sharp cry had just stilled and were waiting for an echo. I would throw myself by her side, breathe strength into her, shield her from suffering. But it would only trouble her more. I know she no longer has the strength to smile in my eyes and give and receive of our marriage.

I prop the picture near the foot of her bed, where she can see it without effort. I sit on the floor, leaning against the rough siding. Without sound or gesture she stares at the painting. While the faint sun shifts patterns on the floor, touches her hair and passes on, she stares. Her eyelashes are wet with tears. When the sun reaches the canvas her hand opens toward me. I move to her side, hold her fingers to my lips. But her eyes are still. Reserved and controlled, she speaks.

"This is how we end, my dearest. I am leaving you. They are coming to take me away today. My daughters. Forever. I have asked them to. Do not speak. Let me say what I can first, or the pain will be too great and I shall never finish. That you hear me and understand me is for me the most important thing in the world."

The rest is dust sifting down on discarded hopes. They have won. Her words come to me detached, as if they were not sounds at all, but tears silently settling on my heart.

"She is so beautiful. Keep her always, promise me you will... I shall not ask you to go with me. You would not, you must not. Even as I tell you that you are wrong, that I now know this, I would have you stay as you are... That's the only truth... Is it selfish of me to say you're wrong? But you must hear it from me. To realize that there may be other ways, that failure is not the end, that there is still sweet wine to be sipped with joy, wine that holds the sun.

"You do not see that I am no longer beautiful. You paint with your heart, not with your eye...and you have shut your wonderful mind away.

"The world does change. It can no longer be fits and starts against a permanent background. And man must learn, perhaps already has learned, to reach—not back into your timelessness, down into the soil, up into the sky, but into new dimensions. You and I do not know what these are. I am leaving to seek them. I can no longer breathe in complete hopelessness... There is no joy left for me. But that is my failure. No, do not torture yourself, my love. It is not you that failed me. Joy is, in the end, solitary. I have lost mine, through weakness or because I am woman and woman is somber and mortal, unable to walk for long with your gods..."

Judge me harshly, Father. Wherever my search rested, my touch was dust. Whoever heard my cry was blighted or perished. The horror in the eyes never dimmed.

Yet I loved her with all the strength I had, and I never loved another. I would have gone with her, abandoned the search, but she was right, my gods would not release me—will they ever? Together, we were both condemned. My touch was dust.

One last account, Father. Of my dear mother—you should hear of my final visit with her. She is still there, in our old house. The garden is gone. High buildings have grown up like weeds on every side, shutting out the light. The windows rattle day and night with the sound of their progress. At first it was slow, though, opposed by the old heart of our town, and she seems hardly to have noticed it. But she never joined, not this. Her causes were often wrong, as you know better than I. Even the last time I saw her she was able to talk of patriotism—and for a country that no longer exists and which was originally created only to destroy. But she has clung to something strong within her and has survived, in her way.

She is a child again. She wears a yellow velvet dress. She is no trouble to others, for she stays at home. She is happy. I, though, I shall join you, before the door quite closes. It will be there for them to read if they care to, the gold lettering... *Extinctus*.

Has it grown so murky that you cannot see me, old man? Come, I am over here, this way, just beyond that line of tombs. You have done well to come here. A beggar has no chance now, with all their organizations and societies and securities, their homes, their prisons. Is it against their law, begging? But you have something for sale. Ah, if only you were the pretty flower girl I once knew! I should buy your whole tray to give to my poor father here who hasn't seen a flower for many years now. Sachets of lavender? Well, never mind, they must do.

Take this. It is all I have. Too much? It is only fair. I have discarded everything, left behind, sold. Even the painting of my lost wife that I hid so long from them. This is the price. It is only right that I in turn give it to you for everything you have.

He shuffles toward the gate of the cemetery, staring at the bundle of bills in his hand. One by one I open the sachets, sprinkle sweet lavender on the tomb.

Released.

Waving cypresses rim my twilight sky. The bats are out now, black scribblings on the fading green glow. I shall lie here by you for a time, Father, rest, for I know my journey now, sleep by you, sleep for a time and go. I have kept one sachet, it is all that I have, it is for her, my dearest wife. I shall find her, she will show me the way.

I have started up into the hills. Behind, is a wasted plain of dust, ahead, a distant peak. It is a desolate withered landscape, greens passing to yellows, browns. There is some growth, though, some life. Here, in a shallow valley of the gradually mounting land, is a small vineyard, untended, leaves turned silver-brown, falling onto the caked earth. Meager bunches of grapes still hang, abandoned. I walk up the last row, near it. I am aware of a denser mass of color stretched halfway up along several of the vines, a rustle, something in the vines close by me. Crawling, on the further side of the row, belly toward me, grasping the vines with two-toed wiry legs, is an enormous insect. Close enough to touch, I can see its dry beak-like mouth snatching eagerly at the few remaining grapes, eating each bunch in one gulp. Its mouth is placed back under its nose, as it were, like a shark. Our eyes meet, brown and yellow eyes like the desolation behind it.

It drops to the ground—the length of two men, the girth of one, the color of the dust. It scuttles down between the rows, comes out into the open, circles wide around me, heading for the hills. Its size is shocking, but by its speed and its dry jiggling motions it seems weightless, a hollow crusty shell on twitching spindles. Off on a path through the dying fields.

I am startled, but without fear, indignant, drawn tight with hate. Destroy it, that which would rob these last fruits of the dying earth! I curse you! Help me! Instantly two men on horseback race by after the insect. I am running too, but they disappear over a rise, into the dust and ruins of the countryside.

I run on, the breath sobbing in me. Not far beyond the rise, I come upon the men. They are dismounted at a fork in the path, their horses standing a few paces off to the side. As I come up to them I notice that they are digging with swords or bayonets. They are dressed in a wild rough sort of uniform. They are digging a trench in the hard black soil by the path. Though I do not turn my eyes from them to look for it, I know they have killed the creature.

"Was it an insect?"

"Yes," they answer me.

"What do you call it?"

"They are called FREQUENTI."

I would ask them more. The name seems odd. But they have turned back to their deliberate melancholy digging.

I move on. Off to the side of the track, hidden before by a rubble of rocks, I see it, a few tangled legs, the back section of the completely severed body, already bleaching in the white sun, its hollowness black, a yellowish-red ooze in the dust.

Should I have dug a trench there too, lain down in my grave forever? I climb on, leaving that behind. Up the slopes. To the mountain's top.

The air is thin here, burned to ozone, too thin and cold for the windpipes of the FREQUENTI. They circle about in the lowlands, multiplying and ravaging, as is their instinct. Lower down I could still hear their scuttlings and chewings and raspings, now blown away by the wind. They can reach me no more.

The sun is fixed at its zenith, the sky embraces me. I am alone, where to stretch, to look into the distance, is to reach and see inward. The external limits are surpassed, the infinite internal opens around me, brilliant, shadowless, to the caress of her gleaming black hair, to the scent of that sweetest wine.

About the Author

BORN IN Boston, Robert Cabot served in the U.S. Army during World War II in England, North Africa, Corsica, the Southern France invasion, Austria, and Germany. With degrees from Harvard and Yale Law School, he served for ten years with the Marshall Plan and foreign aid programs in Italy, Thailand, Sri Lanka, and Washington, D.C. He resigned from the foreign service in protest over U.S. policy in southeast Asia, turning to work with intentional communities, the citizen diplomacy movement, and environmental and social change projects. Writing, however, is his first love. He is the author of a critically acclaimed novel, *The Joshua Tree*, as well as many short pieces and articles. Robert Cabot now lives with his wife and two of his six children in Seattle, Washington and on Whidbey Island. His studio is a thirty-foot sailboat, the sloop *Aeoli*, in which he soloed the Atlantic.